Prayers and Incantations to the Light
Blessings from the Mother

Prayers and Incantations to the Light
Blessings from the Mother

Denise Iwaniw-Francisco

"I need sunlight

I need moonlight

I need stars to *dance*

in my hair."

~ Denise Iwaniw-Francisco

Temple Within Publishing
2017

Copyright 2017 by The Temple Within Publishing,
The Temple Within LLC

This publication is a creative work fully protected by all applicable copyright laws, as well as by misappropriation, trade secret unfair competition, and other applicable laws.

No part of this book may be reproduced in any form without permission in writing from the publisher, except by a reviewer who wishes to quote brief passages in connection with a review written for inclusion in a digital, print, or PDF magazine, periodical or newspaper.

All rights to this publication will be vigorously defended.

The Temple Within LLC 12841 Hillcrest NE, Lowell MI 49331

DeniseIwaniw.com

First Edition 2017©

ISBN: 978-0-9886851-7-8

Graphics: David Fix, Hearth Productions llc, Hearthproductions.com

Editors: Della Badwound, Lillian Cosme, Todd Francisco, Dinah Gerard, Sharon Rosenblum

Back Cover Photo, Equestrian Photo and Head Photo of Denise:

Nicole Werner at NW Photography, Apple Valley, MN

NicoleWernerPhotography.com

New Lakota Dictionary – Lakota Language Consortium

All rights reserved.

A Word from the Editors and Artist

Prayers and Incantations to the Light – Blessings from the Mother, brings a new level of spiritual insight and information to seekers on the spiritual path. Readers will discover why these beautiful prayers and incantations will be treasured. Denise (Dana) Iwaniw-Francisco not only provides vivid accounts of her spiritual journey but educates the reader along the way. Dana's dedication and devotion to the Light as a child, student, teacher, mystic, and Thunder Dreamer are spiritually moving. This divinely timed volume created for the Light Show-ers of today is perfect – surely this volume will be the first of many. It's an honor to know Dana as she continues to share her gifts, wisdom and empowers everyone to shine their light. - *Lillian Cosme*

Prayers and Incantations to the Light – Blessings from the Mother is truly a gift. In the first section, (Dana) Iwaniw-Francisco shares stories from her personal journey that uplift and inspire. She speaks to the path of connectedness and higher calling that await us all when we open to it. The next section serves as a spiritual toolbox, upon which readers can rely and return to again and again. She blankets the reader with varied and magnificent prayers and incantations for every area of life. Stunning photographs from Denise's travels interweave the stories and prayers, offering readers a complete experience of love and light. I am grateful to Denise for the opportunity to edit this wonderful book.

- *Dinah Gerard*

Prayers and Incantations to the Light – Blessings from the Mother offers the guidance we have been looking and hoping for to assist us as we walk Grandmother Earth. The information, prayers and insights are so greatly needed at this time in our world. Dana shares her love for humanity and all life along with the insights she receives from Spirit. The result is a guide for those of us who are open to hearing the messages of love and inspiration; to aid us on our own journey as we walk "The Red Road" - our life on the planet. It has been an honor and a privilege to assist Dana with the editing of this beautiful book. - *Sharon Rosenblum*

It was my honor and pleasure to not only edit *Prayers and Incantations to the Light – Blessings from the Mother*, but to also watch this book germinate in Dana over the past number of years. It was in her, building its way to the surface through each adventurous trip and experience, the great and the rough. Over the years, I've watched her step aside after many of our excursions to sit down and write down key events in her diary, and doodle the visions that were passed along to her. Finally, she felt the time was right and this volume started taking shape. As she was creating this, it continued to evolve, version after version into this wonderful volume that is part auto-biography and part reference material. Just when I would think it was perfect, she would think of something else she needed to add or modify, continuing to develop it into the magnificent gift that it is today. While there are many books that are a great read, but you rarely pick up a second time, except to maybe hand to a friend, this is one of those books you'll keep readily available as reference material or for times when you just want to grab something for a quick read. I've had the pleasure of grabbing this book numerous times, often-times searching for it in her office, flipping through it until I found the exact prayer or incantation that was needed in my life at that time. It's been an absolute pleasure to be part of bringing this together and I am excited that this volume is finally being released out to the world for everyone's enjoyment. Enjoy! - *Todd Francisco*

Denise asked me to create a cover for her book that featured a conjuror, creating love and light. I went through eighteen iterations before Denise and I felt the image was complete. Metatron's Cube, the symbol on the cover, is the template of creation. It contains the feminine circles with the masculine straight lines. Everything that modern science knows about the periodic table of elements are tied together through the five platonic solids, which come out of Metatron's Cube, which is formed from the Fruit of Life, which comes from the Flower of Life. I recommend "The Ancient Secret of the Flower of Life" by Drunvalo Melchizedek for more information about this subject. Searching, "spirit science metatron's cube" will also guide you to quality resources. - *David Fix*

For All Time

"In the beginning,

during the spaces in between,

and ultimately in the end,

we are connected

to every living thing,

seen and *un*seen.

And in every ounce

of each exquisite moment

of this life,

we are loved

beyond all earthly understanding."

-Denise Iwaniw-Francisco

Dedication

This book is dedicated to the Cosmic Mother in all of Her splendid forms, both seen and unseen.

Lady Chapel, Notre Dame du Chartres, Chartres, France 2014

Author's Note

Chartres, France
June 18, 2014

Sitting deep within my prayers to Creator, I heard Her speak to me. In Her loving, yet pointed way, the Mother was instructing me once again, to write. Kneeling in the splendor and perfume of Her goddess energy found well within the stone walls of the magnificent Templar cathedral, Notre Dame de Chartres, she called my soul to listen.

"Dana, you shall name this epistle, *Prayers and Incantations to the Light – Blessings from the Mother.* Help my children remember how much they are loved."

"Help my children remember how much they are loved." Those words joyfully haunt me, each and every day.

One year earlier and thousands of miles away, on the Cheyenne River Reservation in South Dakota, I heard these very same words. They were spoken to me inside the sanctuary of another holy place, while I stood within the cedar round house that contains the original pipe bundle of White Buffalo Calf Woman. The sacred smell of sage was in the air as was the loving presence of our Mother.

Resting on the kneeler in Chartres Cathedral, my heart and mind full of the Mother's love, I promised to follow her instruction. It wasn't long before the work ensued.

As if by magic, this manuscript began to unfold while driving across the mystical lands of the Carcassonne region of France. With the magnificence of an eagle flying overhead, the words of the Mother began to course through my hands and onto the blank pages of my small, well-worn travel journal.

And what of the words, *prayer* and *incantations*? Why those words, and what do they truly mean?

By simple definition, the word prayer typically represents a petition to the Creator. It also reflects a desire to have a communion with, gratitude toward, or a specially worded devotion to the Divine Maker and all aspects of It. For many, prayer is also a two-way street of communication in which one prays, and then observes silence in order to receive communication from the Divine in return.

According to the Merriam-Webster Dictionary:

Function: *noun*

Definition of PRAYER

a   (1) : an address (as a petition) to God or a god in word or thought <said a *prayer* for the success of the voyage>

    (2): a set order of words used in praying

b   (1): an earnest request or wish

    (2): the act or practice of praying to God or a god <kneeling in *prayer*>

Incantation on the other hand, is more alchemical in nature. The recitation of incantations or invocations, when performed in a loving and meaningful way, brings about beautiful interaction with the Spirit of all things.

According to the Merriam-Webster Dictionary:

Function: *noun*

Definition of INCANTATION

: a series of words used to make something magical happen

: a use of spells or verbal charms spoken or sung as a part of a ritual of magic; *also*: a written or recited formula of words designed to produce a particular effect.

In my work, co-creating "The Mysteries of Ancient Egypt Empowerment Deck," with artist David Fix, I discovered a magnificent, ancient teaching regarding the importance of maintaining integrity in our thoughts and words. This particular lesson is associated with the Egyptian deity known as Ptah:

"Prayers and incantations, when delivered with integrity through a loving heart, and with the greatest and highest good of *all* in mind, brings about miracles and wonders both great and small. In concert with the Universe and every living thing, loving prayers and incantations bring us that much closer to our understanding of, and our relationship with the Light of the Mother, which is found in all living things."

May the prayers and incantations within this volume supply nourishment for your soul.

Contents

Table of Contents

Prayers and Incantations to the Light..1
Journal Entries...7
    About the Journal Entries
    Becoming Blue Thunder Woman
    Praying with Ptesáwiŋ, White Buffalo Calf Woman
    The Love of Grandmother Willow
    Living a Holy Human Life
    Isis the Loving Mother and the Case of Tomfoolery in the Valley of the Kings
    Emancipation
    What of Prayer
    Prayers for Mní Wičhóni – Sacred and Life Giving Waters
    About My Moccasins, Our Star Ancestors and the Lakota Star Quilt
    UFOs and Star People
    Spiritual Gifts
    My Philosophy of Light
    Haŋbléčheyapi: Vision Quest
    Wolf: Spirit Guardian and Teacher
    It's All a Numbers Game
    The Dark Night and the Light of a Brand New Day
    To Everything There Is a Season
    Awakening from Spiritual Slumber
    Šúŋkawakȟáŋ Wówakȟaŋ: Sacred Horse Medicine
    My Pilgrimage to Chateau de Montsegur
    The Uniqueness of Your Soul
    Planting Seeds

Creating Sacred Spaces for Prayer and Ceremony...62
Prayers...65
    Prayer to Our Lady of the Light
    Blue Thunder Prayer
    Sacred Waters
    Healing the Past
    Releasing That Which No Longer Serves the Path of My Soul
    Warrior's Prayer
    Prayer for Veterans
    Prayer for the Land

    Prayer for World Peace
    Prayer for a Gentle Transition
    Prayer for a Restless Spirit
    Prayer for Entering the Dreamworld
    Releasing Worry
    Gratitude
    Prayer for Mealtime
    Healing Addictions
    Prayer for Sobriety
    Healing Ancestral Trauma
    Healing Cellular Memories
    Prayer for the Animals
    Horse Nation Prayer
    Morning Prayer
    Mid-Day Prayer
    Evening Prayer
    Restorative Sleep
    Prayer for Strength and Courage
    A Heart That Is Open
    An Open Mind
    An Open Third Eye
    Receiving
    Light in the Mourning
    Banishing Negativity
    Death Without Dying

Incantations..**109**
    Incantation to the Mother – Litany of Her Holy Names
    Incantation to the Goddess – She Who Has Many Faces and Names
    The Alchemy of Incantations and the Sacred Directions............................112
        Incantation to the Light of the Seven Directions
        Seven Sacred Winds
        The Four Winds
    Mother Nature..119
        Incantation to the Spirits of Nature
        Incantation to the Sun
        Incantation to the Moon
        Incantation to the Stars – The Litany of Mystical Light
    Caring for Sacred Objects..124
        Incantation to Clear and Recharge Crystals

Incantation to Bless a Sacred Object
Incantation to the Faerie Realms
Incantation to the Spirit of Love
Incantation to the Ancestors
Incantation to the Inner Elementals
Incantation to the Four Seasons
Incantation to the Five Ethers

The Nine Orders of Angels..*134*
Incantation to the Nine Orders of Angels

The Four Mighty Archangels..*136*
Incantation to the Four Mighty Archangels

The Creation of Sacred Waters..*138*
Creating Holy Water
Calling to the Angelics

Chakras..*141*
Protecting Your Energy Body
Incantation to the Seven Chakras
Incantation to the Divine Intelligence Within My Body
Incantation to My Higher Self and Soul

Prayers and Ceremonies for Rites of Passage..**149**
Prayers for a Baptismal Rite
Prayer for Welcoming a Child to Their Earthly Journey
Prayer to Bless a Child
Naming Ceremony

End of Life and Funeral Rites..**155**
Celebration of Life Ceremony
Prayer for the Journey Home
Prayer for Homecoming
Upon the Four Winds I Commend Your Spirit
Prayer for the Passing of a Beloved Pet

Weddings and Partnership Rites..**167**
Ceremony of Sacred Union
Wedding Ceremony
Invitation to the Angels of Love
Calling to the Winds of Union

Epilogue..**174**

Notes

Table of Sacred Geometry

Merkaba..**Title Page**

Mer means Light. Ka means Spirit. Ba means Body. The Merkabah is a vehicle that can be used to travel to or connect with the higher realms.

Sagittarius...**xv**

Sagittarius represents idealism. People with this sign joyously travel seeking meaning in life. They are social and optimistic and have the ability to transform their goals into reality.

Scorpio...**xvi**

Scorpio represents passionate determination. People with this sign are extremely determined and true. They value long-term friendships and are excellent keepers of secrets.

Pisces..**5**

Pisces represents romance. People with this sign are compassionate and intuitive. They earn and maintain friendships by being selfless and empathetic.

Sulfur..**6**

Sulfur represents balance and protection. It is associated with the complexity of human nature and our ability to transcend and reach enlightenment.

Aquarius...**8**

Aquarius represents independence. People with this sign use intellectual thought to aid in progressing forward. They enjoy helping others and are natural problem solvers.

Saturn..**44**

Saturn represents death and rebirth. It is associated with agriculture and with the harvest. It also represents strength and supreme willpower.

Aries..**45**

Aries represents the beginning of something. As such, people with this sign crave to be first and are natural leaders. They are dynamic and eager to take action.

Virgo..**46**

Virgo represents carefulness. People with this sign methodically pay attention to details. They are well-organized and prefer to delve deep into minutia others might find trivial.

Mercury...**49**

Mercury represents swift transformation. It is associated with using thoughts to manifest quickly. It also represents freedom of thought and inventiveness.

Capricorn..**61**

Capricorn represents responsibility. People with this sign are often serious and self-disciplined. They have a great ability to lead others and learn from their mistakes. They value family and tradition.

Taurus..**64**

Taurus represents stability. People with this sign are reliable and seek to faithfully complete projects and goals. They are sometimes strong-willed, protective and materialistic as they are an earth sign.

Libra..**107**

Libra represents diplomacy. People with this sign are gracious and cooperative. They are peace-keepers who crave balance and fairness.

Gemini...**108**

Gemini represents two personalities. People with this sign can be very fun and witty one moment, and very serious the next. They feel like half of them is missing, so they connect easily with others.

Leo...**117**

Leo represents the king of the jungle. People with this sign are self-confident and dramatic natural leaders. They attract many friends with whom they are loyal and generous.

Medicine Wheel..**118**

The Medicine Wheel is sometimes referred to as the Scared Hoop in Native American traditions. It is used in ceremonies for healing. It also symbolizes the movements of the sun and the stages of life.

Moon..**147**

The moon is a feminine sign that is associated with cycles and rhythm. It represents immortality and sometimes the darker, mysterious side of human nature.

Salt...**148**

Salt represents the bond of a deep friendship. As such, it symbolizes the sacred. It also is used in ceremonies for protection.

Cancer...**154**

Cancer represents sentimental loyalty to family. People with this sign tend to be emotional and crave deep attachments to others. They are very loyal and easily empathize with others.

Sun...**165**

The sun represents the mind and intellect. It is associated with the cosmic power and a dominant male force. It also represents seeing and vision.

Tree of Life..**166**

The Tree of Life represents immortality. It is associated with personal growth and is associated with wisdom, strength, beauty and protection.

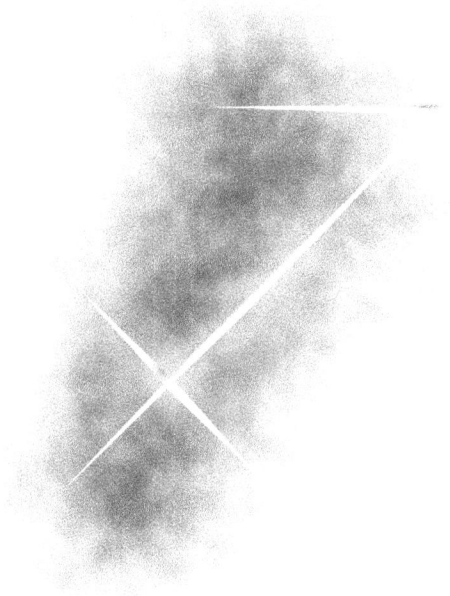

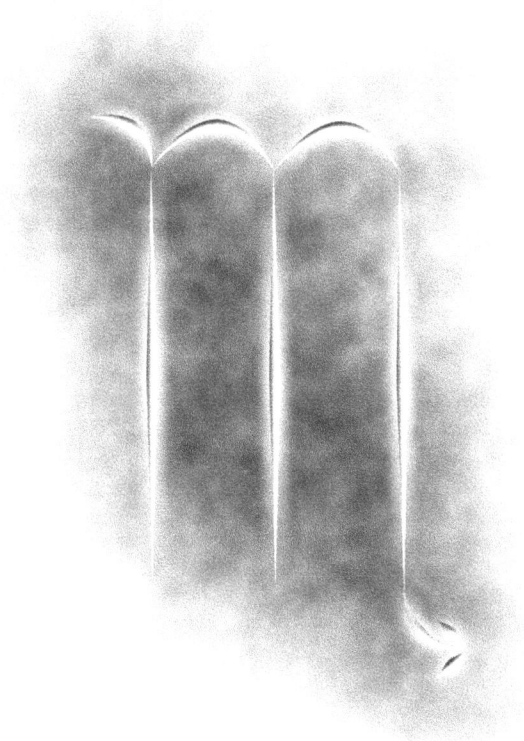

Prayers and Incantations to the Light

Pathway to the Cave of St. Mary Magdalene, St. Baume, France 2014

The Mother loves us. She is ever reaching out to us through the invisible veils and octaves that seemingly separate us from Her loving splendor.

As a young child and a developing mystic, I was keenly aware of the Holy Mother's presence in my life. While I had no way to adequately verbalize this sense of knowing, I simply *knew* that I was never, ever alone. Mary, as I was taught to call her, had been with me from the dawn of my earthly journey and surely, I felt, was never to leave my side.

She comforted me as my spiritual gifts began to unfold at a very young and tender age. Ghostly apparitions, and visitations that were sometimes quite terrifying, often found me hiding under my covers, praying for relief from the onslaught of unwelcome spirit communications. Oftentimes in tears and shaking from the nightly encounters, it was Mary who would come to settle my young heart and send my uninvited guests away. Like a warm presence in the center of my chest, I could feel Our Lady touch me. With that touch, my five-year-old heart and my racing mind could, once again, find peace.

So began my quest to fully realize and understand my relationship with the Mediatrix of Heaven and Earth, the Queen of the Sun, Moon and Stars.

Mine has been a lifetime of deep and sacred love for Her love; the love of the Mother. From my extensive travels and experiences toward Her, in the Temples of Isis at Philae and Abydos; the Queens Chamber of the Great Pyramid at Giza; the Abbey and Chalice Well in Glastonbury; the sacred monoliths of Stonehenge, and Carnac; the birthing stones on the island of Kaua'i; the Abbey ruins on the Isle of Iona in Scotland; Merlin's Cave in Tintagel; the White Eagle Lodge in London; the Hag Stone and ancient cairns of Ireland, Montsegur, Rocamadour and Chartres in France; to the round house of the White Buffalo Calf Pipe in South Dakota; Holy Hill Shrine in Wisconsin and the Sweetgrass Hills of Montana; I have discovered that there is a single element that perfumes these holy places, threading them together like a sacred sutra. It is the essence of unconditional, abiding love.

Life has taught me that *all* things are alive with the sacred breath of the Creator; and to varying degrees include both the male and female expressions of the One True Light. For far too long, the divine Mother has been shrouded in mystery, ignorance and the slumber of forgotten Truths.

It is only when we learn to *see*, as the seer sees, to *listen* as the wise elder listens and *feel* as the mystics feel that we begin to truly experience the Light of the Mother in all living things, including ourselves.

For many years I have attempted to write and collate a book of prayers and sacred incantations that would help me to part this veil. Starts were made and quickly died. Each attempt at a manuscript, was in its own way, an initiation, another lesson in Divine timing and the need to let Spirit lead the way when writing about the Sacred.

On June 18, 2014 my soul led me to Chartres, France and to its Templar Cathedral, dedicated to the Ascending Mother, the rising of the Goddess.

It was in this Temple to the Rising Sun that I found myself kneeling on the ancient wooden rails of the Lady Chapel, my shoulders draped in the royal purple scarf that I had purchased in Cairo, Egypt in 2009, having yet another heart-to-Sacred Heart conversation with the Holy Mother, Mary.

From a sacred and ancient place deep within me, I heard Her whispering to my heart, "Dana, the title of your epistle shall be, "Prayers and Incantations to the Light (Blessings from the Mother)."

Tears filled my eyes and spilled down my cheeks in warm, loving streams as we continued our dialogue.

"Mother," I asked, "why has it taken so long for this book to come to fruition, when my attempts began so long ago?"

Kindly, reassuringly, Our Lady of Grace responded to my heartfelt question. "It was necessary for your soul's growth and divine avocation that you were to come back here to France, Dana. Like so many of the sacred places around the earth that are dedicated to the understanding of Me, this holy, mystery school temple called to your spirit and your soul answered. You have traveled within these hallowed temple walls in lifetimes past, and I have beckoned you here once more. Look around you. Remember. My divine names are many, and my face is recognized uniquely by each. My voice is riding an ascending wave that is now reaching a crescendo throughout the vastness of the universe. The Mother longs to hold Her children in the Light of this new day, once more."

Unbeknownst to me and at this very point in my silent dialogue, two friends, sitting just outside the lady-chapel, gazing in, began to hear what both would later describe to me as the singing of a choir of Angels. So profound and unexplainable was the experience, that both women were moved to tears.

As my conversation with the Divine Mother came to a close, I was blanketed in a feeling that I described as a blue, starry love. Celestial, all-embracing love. I gave thanks.

With a final word, *She* reminded me that *She* would guide my pen and my heart throughout the course of creating this manuscript and in the culmination of the prayers and incantations that I would receive in the comings weeks and months.

Dabbing at the moisture still fresh under my lashes, I crossed myself and stood to return to my friends who were caught up in the beauty and union of this moment with the Mother.

When we were at last able to put voice to our experiences, we shared what we were able. Slowly and reverently we made our way to the labyrinth which was, as it has been for centuries, located in the center of the cathedral, embedded into its ancient, stony floor.

Removing our shoes, we stood upon the six-petaled rose, located in the center of the labyrinth. The very petals that had been touched by Templar Knights and pilgrims alike, for over seven centuries.

The cool tingling began at the bottoms of my feet, slowly ascending upward through my legs, my thighs, until it reached the place of my Inner Sun, the solar plexus, and began to warm. Ultimately, this now warm and tingly energy rose upward to the center of my heart.

"Remember, Dana, to carry the Light so that others may *see*. Hold it high so that others will find their way to Me." I felt Her grace dancing within the starry, blue octaves that now filled my entire being.

My moment with the Divine was heightened by excited shouts that were coming toward me and my friends. "Dana! I found the iron nail!" It was my husband Todd, anxiously arriving at the labyrinth to let us all know that he had discovered the solstice stone that contains the Templar nail. Denoting the precise spot within the Templar cathedral that marks the rising summer solstice sun at noon in Gemini, the nail and the symbology of its message is legendary. The rising sun. The Ascending Mother. The return of the female to Her rightful place in the Heart and Mind of the World.

In silent anticipation, our small group followed Todd back to the stone and the nail, each taking a turn placing our hands upon it and receiving a blessing from the Sun.

So it is that I dedicate this book to the Mother and the Sun and the Spirit of the Holy Light that resides within all living things.

By whatever name you call them, when held in sacred balance, the wonders and miracles of the universe, including you are revealed.

It is my wish that the personal stories, travel photos, journal entries, and prayers and incantations within these written pages, will bring a joyful peace to your heart, a loving relationship with all of creation and wonderment to your days.

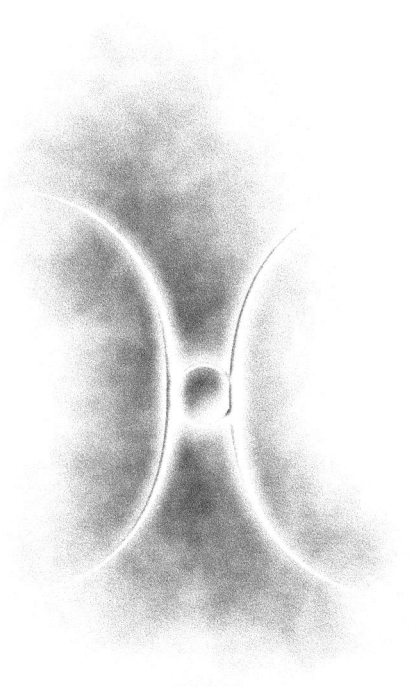

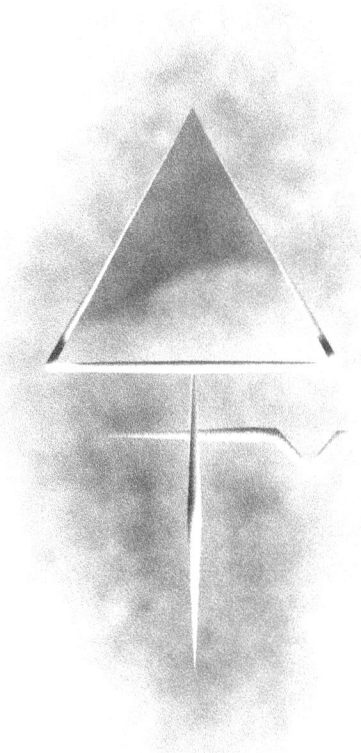

Journal Entries

Reliquary of St. Mary Magdalene inside the cave of her refuge and passing,
St. Baume, France, 2014

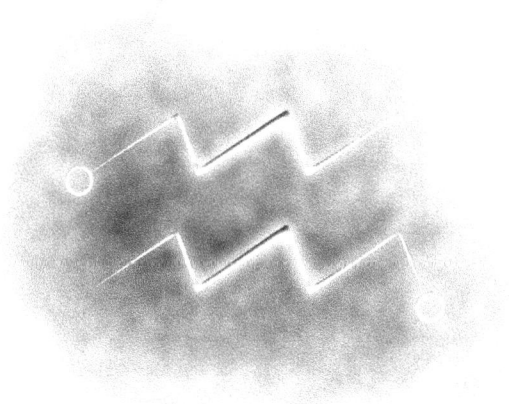

About the Journal Entries

Church of the Apparition, Cairo, Egypt, 2009

Recollections of deeply meaningful moments with Spirit, and my fellow human adventurers are contained within the upcoming pages that I have entitled quite simply, *Journal Entries.*

For decades now, it has been customary for me to record in my private journals the many explorations that my soul has taken me on. Detailing the conversations, sights, sounds, smells, tastes and interactions that I experienced while on my travels around Grandmother Earth is cathartic for me.

As a firm believer that every encounter is a holy encounter, and that everything happens for a reason, chronicling gives me opportunity to reflect, digest and grow in the understanding that my life and the work of my soul has a purpose. I often visualize myself as a single strand of Light that is radiating forward from the heart and mind of Creator, destined to intermingle with other strands of living beings of Light, in order to experience the passion of human life.

The journal entries are not in any particular order. They are chronicled here as Spirit inspired me to do so.

Many years ago, I asked one of my Lakota Sioux elder teachers about the protocol for publicly sharing the sacred events in my life. Here is the wisdom that he imparted to me. "Denise, your life is your story. Share your stories. They may help people learn more about themselves or their relationship with the Great Spirit. It is not up to you to share the stories of *others*, only those stories that are your own and the stories that you have been asked to share."

Of the hundreds of diary entries that exist in my continually growing collection, I have been moved to include more than 20 of them in this book. Some may seem rather mundane, while others may appear to be a bit fantastical. I humbly offer them so that you might experience a sense of wonder, camaraderie and a deeper understanding of your personal experiences with Creator.

Becoming Blue Thunder Woman

For most of my life, *answering the call* was something that I believed happened to other people. Men or women destined for the clergy always came to the forefront of my mind when I heard people talk about *the call.* Even today, when I think of those words, I envision God on one end of a telephone line dialing up from somewhere in the starry nations and the recipient of heaven's divine marching orders picking up the phone receiver here on planet earth, reveling in a moment of divine ecstasy as their soul's avocation was being revealed to them from on high.

My understanding of *the call* changed in 2006. The preconceived notions that I held for so many decades came to a screeching halt when I heard these words, which were spoken to me by an elder Lakota Sioux heyókȟa holy man, "White Owl Woman told me you were coming. I found you here in Michigan. She just whispered into my ear that you are the one. Your life is about to change and I am going to teach you the medicine ways."

Except for the brilliant streams of light being emitted from the stars, the sky was a dark, inky blue. The sacred fire cast shadows across the holy grounds and into the doorway of the sweat lodge, where he and I sat and I received my very own *call from Creator.*

For eight nights in a row, we were participating in sweat ceremonies with him near my home in West Michigan. He was in Michigan, at the invitation of a woman who had recently become my friend.

During the second evening of sweat lodges, before sacred ceremony even began, the medicine man took me aside to tell me that Spirit had told him to begin preparing me for the responsibility of carrying the 'čhaŋnúŋpa wakȟáŋ' (sacred pipe). As part of the preparations, he was instructed to make me one of his relatives in the ancient Lakota Sioux way of the huŋká káǧA ceremonial rite. He shared with me that months earlier he had been told by Spirit that he would be meeting a woman who he was to bring into the medicine ways. He also shared that he was surprised when spirit told him *that* woman was me, because I am not of full blood Lakota lineage. The spirits however, were clear in telling him that my Blackfeet and Kiowa ancestry was calling me to the Red Road and that he was to follow what Creator had intended.

As the second round of the 'inípi', or sweat lodge, began, a spirit being presented itself inside the darkness of the lodge and began to speak very loudly to me. So loud in fact, that my daughter Elyse, who was thirteen years old at the time and sitting next to me in the inky blackness, could also hear the spirit speaking over the singing and sacred drumming that was happening inside the sweat lodge. With her eyes wide as saucers and my heart beating very quickly, we heard the discarnate speak, "Tonight you are receiving your spirit name. Did you hear me? Tonight you are receiving your spirit name! Your name is Wakiŋyaŋ Tȟó Wiŋyaŋ, Blue Thunder Woman. Do you understand what I am saying?" All I could muster in response to this boisterous spirit being was, "Yes, I understand."

When the second round of the sweat lodge came to a conclusion, the holy man announced that the spirits had given me a spirit name and then he shared that name with everyone inside the sweat lodge. At that point, he and his wife, accompanied by another medicine man and his wife, exited the lodge and stood just outside the inípi and next to the hocoka wakan, the sacred altar. The medicine man called to me, "Wakiŋyaŋ Tȟó Wiŋyaŋ, please come out here. Spirit has asked me to perform the making of the relatives now. We will perform the huŋká káǧA and you will become our relative."

Stepping out into the cool, starlit night, soft embers from the fire still glowing several feet from me, I was greeted by the two medicine men and their wives. As the holy men sang and prayed the sacred songs of this rite in the ancient Lakota language, the women welcomed me into their family as a relative and in the tradition of this official adoption ceremony, they tied an eagle plume into my hair.

My tipi

When the rite was complete and the five of us entered back into the lodge, I was now their relative, each of us bound to the other, in a sacred Lakota way.

"Your spiritual path finds you, you don't find it." This is a spiritual teaching that I heard for decades, but hadn't really understood until that crisp autumn evening in November of 2006. Nor was I fully prepared for the wondrously intense and spiritually exhaustive medicine journey that would begin because of it. My path on the 'Čhaŋkú Lúta' (Red Road) had officially begun.

Receiving *the call* was very different than I had supposed it would ever be. My rational, Western mind railed against the message, but my heart … well, my heart welcomed it. My soul recognized the moment and cried out in sacred recollection of that holy instant. Together, my heart and soul embraced *the calling* as a long-lost friend who had suddenly returned after many years of painful absence. Tears fell uncontrollably, yet silently.

Solemn, life-worn faces presenting themselves to me in night time apparitions were a common event in my youth. Countless visits by the specters of Native American men, unknown to me at that time, had been preparing me for this very moment. In my attempt to understand them and their silent messages, I sat at my bedroom desk and drew their face in charcoals, and pastels on a sketch paper pad. Each man appeared to me, like a long lost friend who had come to sit a spell and comfort me. They *did* comfort me. I shared their visitations and my art with no one.

More than three decades later, they appeared once again. Under the starlit sky they stood with me and bore witness to their voiceless messages coming full circle.

Worries about what the neighbors, friends, family members or my corporate co-workers might think, were of no concern to me. *The Call* erases all fears. It assures us that Creator is supporting us, bidding us forward on our Path. The heart and soul see and feel and *know* that there is no turning back, except at the risk of losing our way and our Self.

Answering *the call* requires us to leave the 'old' us behind in order to for us to grow into the fullness of our Being. It means that embracing change is a must and allowing the future to unfold in divine timing is completely and utterly necessary. The journey of receiving, embracing, unfolding and walking the path of our unique soul is the reason for our earth journey. *The calling* is received in many ways, and yet each of us receives it during our earthly life. The choice however, to answer *the call* or not, is ours to make.

In the years since receiving *the call* my life has changed vastly and yet I couldn't imagine it any other way. The tailored designer suits, matching pumps and handbags are long gone. The sacred pipe, sun dance and sweat lodges have replaced them and they've helped me to grow as a spiritual being and as a human being, in a way that fine suits, pumps and handbags never could.

Life does not grow easier by answering *the call*. It grows in depth, sacred knowledge and divine wisdom. Most importantly, it cultivates our connection to Creator and all living things. It brings us to the realization that we are in all, and all is within us.

Balancing my Catholic upbringing with the Red Road Way of Life as a sacred pipe carrier has been for me, quite easy. Removing religious dogma and seeing the commonalities in mystical teachings, has been a beautiful dovetail for both worlds to collectively teach and lead me.

In both traditions, I am known as a Thunder Dreamer; a Seer. I'm often asked what those words mean. In esoteric terms, they simply mean that I see beyond the veil and that I reflect what I see. I was called to answer that question as a keynote speaker at the 2015 Great Dakota Gathering in Winona, Minnesota:

"I am a Thunder Dreamer.

I reflect. I repel. I reveal. I invite.

I see.

Like the sacred breath of the universes, cosmos, stars, suns and moons, the spirit of the thunder and lightning are also contained within me. They are my deepest allies in my walk through shadow and light.

When the Thunder Dreamer appears, what once was needed is laid to rest. What is yet necessary to your earthly journey still remains.

Every encounter with the sacred seer is a holy encounter; a time to die and a good day to be born again."

I am and I continue to be, trained by Lakota elders, my adopted family of Lakota Sioux elders, in the tradition of the *western door* ways…the direction of the thunderers, mystics, many deaths without dying, and the realm of the ancestors.

"Denise, your medicine does not come from another medicine man or woman,

it comes from within yourself. It is a gift from Wakan Tanka."

Wilmer "Buzz" Young Man Afraid of His Horses

Praying with Ptesáwiŋ

She is called by many names; Ptesáwiŋ, White Buffalo Calf Woman…and Mother.

In August of 2014, I had the humble honor of spending time once again on the Cheyenne River Reservation with Chief Arvol Looking Horse, the 19th Generational Keeper of the White Buffalo Calf Bundle. While I have spent other occasions for ceremony there at his home in South Dakota, this particular ceremonial event was one that I had only dreamed I would one day be part of.

At the conclusion of Chief Looking Horse's annual Sundance ceremony, She would be removed from the security of her log round house and brought out amongst the People so that they could pray and be with Her. The sacred bundle, containing Her gift of the original 'čhaŋnúŋpa wakȟáŋ' or sacred prayer pipe, is brought out only once a year. To my great fortune, Spirit saw to it that I would be a participant and a soul witness to this most sacred of ceremonies.

Before the pipe came out into the light of day, each man and woman needed to be prepared by purification in the inípi, or sweat lodge, before praying with the sacred bundle. Men would be cleansed in a male lodge and women in a lodge poured by a female lodge keeper. I'm not certain how many lodge rounds I poured that beautiful summer morning, but I savored each and every one of them knowing that by doing so, I was participating in a sacred rite that was also given to us by the White Buffalo Calf Woman, long, long ago. At the time Ptesáwiŋ gifted the very first pipe to those two Lakota warriors on the Great Plains of Turtle Island, 19 generations ago, she also gave us the purification ceremony, called inípi.

When all of the men and women who would pray with the bundle were purified, a thick trail of South Dakota sage was laid down by my husband, Todd. While I poured lodges that morning, Todd picked fresh sage for several hours, in order that the ceremonial trail would be as it has always been, laden with the sacred medicine of sage. This long and winding road of sage ran from the Sundance arbor way up to the round house, located on a hill perched above the ceremonial Sundance grounds. The ancient White Buffalo Calf Bundle would be carried by members of the Looking Horse family from the top of the hill, and down into the Sundance arbor.

With the trail now properly prepared, each of us sacred pipe carriers was called into the center of the Sundance ceremony grounds to load our čhaŋnúŋpa wakȟáŋ with white willow or 'čhaŋšáša' and then re-wrap them in their red cloths. We would bring our pipes with us when we prayed with the White Buffalo Calf Bundle, leaving them wrapped and unsmoked. Chief Looking Horse asked us to bring these loaded pipes home to our friends and families and to share them with those we love. In doing so, we would be sharing the love of Ptesáwiŋ.

From the moment that the door to the round house opened by Arvol, her energy enveloped us. A wave of mothering, wise and loving energy unlike anything I've experienced permeated what felt like the entire universe around all of us. As She made her way down the hill, along the sage trail, we sang Her song. With all of our heart and with all of our soul, we sang to acknowledge Her. It is the very same čhaŋnúŋpa wakȟáŋ prayer that we sing each time our prayer pipes are loaded in my inípi. An ancient lullaby that welcomes Her presence into our ceremonies and into our lives.

Following Her and the Looking Horse family down into the Sundance arbor was unspeakably beautiful. Not long after, Todd and I found ourselves side by side, on our knees and hugging the buffalo robed bundle that contains the original altar for the People. My pipe resting gently upon Her, I prayed within the silence of my heart; "Mother, you know what is in my heart and what is in my mind. Make me an instrument of your peace on Grandmother Earth. Guide my steps and my words. Thank you for keeping me on the Good Red Road. Thank you for loving me."

It was within the silence of my heart that She spoke to me and showed me visions of things to come. To this day, and even while writing this column I find it difficult to adequately describe what it was like to pray with Ptesáwiŋ. The visions, I keep within my heart.

How do we describe the indescribable?

Many times I have started to write these thoughts and many times I have tossed them away.

When we ask for Her to be present with us, She is. White Buffalo Calf Woman loves each and every living thing, with a mother's heart. In this time of the return of peace and the spirit of 'mitákuye oyáš'iŋ' (we are all related) upon Grandmother Earth, Ptesáwiŋ asks you to remember that all children around Grandmother Earth are our children, just as you are one of Hers.

White Buffalo Calf Woman tells us that we must do more than just say the words, we must walk them. Most importantly, she reminds us to be young at heart and walk our path with love for all things. In that way, we are the living and loving expression of the Great Spirit on earth.

The Love of Grandmother Willow

I heard the old, gnarled willow call my name as I stood in front of the Young Girls Dormitory. The now dilapidated building that once housed hundreds of precious young Anishinabe girls, most as  young as five, had tugged on my heart strings from across the boarding school campus. Sitting not far from the gymnasium whose exterior bricks bear the energy of the students who carved their names into them, and whose voices still ring across the wooden gym floors and rows of wooden chairs and benches, sits this dormitory for the very young. Peering into the partially boarded up windows, I could still hear their innocent chatter, their cries for help and feel their longing for family and home. My eyes and my heart wept for their longing. My soul prayed that at the end of their earthly existence, they were reunited with those who never saw their return from the boarding school; family members who themselves died of broken hearts and unspeakable poverty as they waited for the return of a child, a beloved child that ultimately never returned.

"Come here Blue Thunder Woman, come here." Called a gentle voice from behind the run down brick building.

"Come visit with me and let me tell you about the children who once came here."

Following the sound of this soothing voice, I slowly made my way around the Young Girls Dormitory, across a small patch of grassy land, to a place and an experience that is forever etched on my heart.

As they walked up behind me, hand in hand, I heard the voice of an Anishinabe tribal elder speak those words to her teenage granddaughter.

"Do you see those large old knots there on Grandmother Willow? If you look closely, you will see that they look like the faces of children. Our elders tell us that the reason they look that way is that when the young children died here at this boarding school, Grandmother Willow took them into herself to make their journey back home to Creator safe and loving. Their beautiful faces are a permanent reminder to us of what happened here."

Moments earlier, as I gazed at those faces etched in bark and offered my prayers of gratitude to Grandmother Willow, Spirit had already whispered those same thoughts into my heart and mind. In her lifetime, she helped more than 240 children walk on from this sterile place. As their young souls left their earthly bodies from disease, lack of nurturing and abuse, Grandmother held them in her own living body, assisting them on their journey upward, back to the star nations, their ancestors and into the loving arms of the Creator who gave them life. Her gnarly, yet tender and ancient body remains on the boarding school grounds as their story teller and the keeper of loves' Wisdom. As long as she exists, the legacy of the little ones who passed from this life, live on deep within her roots and deep into the starry skies. For all those who gaze upon her and listen to her voice, their legacy lives on within our hearts.

(There is an extraordinary event that takes places in the very heart of the state of Michigan each spring. Along with the warm breezes, fully blossomed trees and the arrival of the dragonflies comes a day of prayer and remembrance. An entire day dedicated to sacred ceremony for all of the youth that once attended and many of whom perished at the Mount Pleasant Indian Industrial School, which operated from June 30, 1893 until June 6, 1934. In 2015, I was invited by Anishinabe tribal elders to participate in a sacred pipe ceremony to honor these souls. The experience was profoundly moving and for me, life changing.)

Shine

"The *brightest* Lights

are sometimes called to shine

in the *darkest* of places."

-Denise Iwaniw-Francisco

Living a Holy Human Life

Sitting within the indelible image of a burnished pink and lavender South Dakota sunset, I am humbled and blessed to be composing these words from the sacred lands of the Cheyenne River Indian Reservation.

"If you wanted to live such a 'wakȟáŋ' holy life, then you should have stayed in the Spirit world! You are wasting a perfectly good human body by not experiencing human life. There are many in the Spirit world who wish they could be here to experience being human. We need to walk the good Red Road, but we need to remember that we also need to do what we came here to do … be human, with human emotions and thoughts and experiences."

The elder was talking to each and every one us about having a spiritual practice or living a spiritual life and maintaining balance between the heavenly and the earthly. "Many times," he said, "people find a spiritual way of life and feel they need to be holy 24 hours a day, seven days a week. They are afraid that if they make mistakes, show emotion, fall off the path, they have failed Creator."

From the moist eyes and smiles all around the arbor, it was clear that his words were striking a heart chord within each of us, opening a space for personal healing and growth to occur.

"My addiction began at 8 years old when my older brothers gave me a half cup of whiskey and told me that I was old enough to begin learning about life," he continued. "Thirty years later, after nearly dying from alcohol and drug addiction, I found myself on the good Red Road of spirituality. Every day, I tried to be holy in everything I did, and every word that I spoke. My friends and family began to make fun of me. They accused me of getting sober and thinking that I was now a heyókȟa man, or spiritual leader. Believe me, being a medicine man was the furthest thing from my mind. That was the point however, when I met the 'wičháša wakȟáŋ', holy man, who gave me the words of wisdom that I just shared with you."

His humble manner, and the tone and cadence of his voice are still with me as I type these words. The Lakota elder spoke to us of a great, yet simple truth and I am changed because of it.

Whether we are spiritual leaders, practitioners, teachers, students or masters, the experience of being holy while being wholly human can bring us to a place of confusion about which is the more altruistic and God pleasing path…holy or human.

The origin of our soul is holy. It is sacred. Our holy and sacred soul chose to incarnate within the confines of flesh and bones. We wanted to experience humanness while expressing the Light of our sacred source, right here on 'Uŋčí Makȟá' Grandmother Earth. In our humanness, we make mistakes, we laugh, we cry, we have joy and love. We experience illness, death, passion and birth. We fall, get up, learn and grow. And all the while, we are, by virtue of the source of our being, holy. We are holy beings, called to shine and experience being wholly human.

Buffalo Skull Altar

Signs and Wonders

"To the one

with eyes to *see*,

ears to *hear*,

and a heart to *feel*,

the entire *universe* is a

sacred tapestry of endless signs

and miraculous wonders."

-*Denise Iwaniw-Francisco*

Isis the Loving Mother

and a Case of Tomfoolery in the Valley of the Kings

If it's true that life is full of teachers and that we often learn through challenging times, the tomb of Thutmosis IV in the Valley of the Kings, Egypt proved to contain teachers, Angels, and unsuspecting rescuers of the most exceptional kind.

"Dana, beware of tomfoolery during your visit to Egypt." Thus began the conversation with my friend, Lisa.

She continued. "While you are there, dark forces are going to try and extinguish your life. Be cautious at all times and protect yourself. Promise me you will be on guard, Dana."

Responding to what I thought was simply an overly concerned friend, I said, "Of course I will, Lisa. Thank you for sharing your dream with me and for taking the time to call." Five months after that conversation, I found myself in ancient Egypt. Specifically, I found myself, along with a dozen others in our travel group, standing in the magnificent Valley of the Kings. Like most foreigners who, for the first time, witness the vast expanse of the sand made mountain range that once contained the human relics and royal treasurers of the Pharaoh's, I was in awe.

Although the mummies and dynastic riches had long since been removed to museums, the fantastic hieroglyphic art depicting the story of their lives and deaths, along with their mammoth sarcophaguses, still remained within each individual tomb.

While many in my group wished to see the tombs of King Tut, and Ramses IX, my soul longed to visit the tomb of Thutmosis IV, the 18th Dynasty ruler of Egypt, sometimes known as the Dreamer.

My rational brain didn't have a reason as to why I would want to hike up the side of a steep mountain to visit the tomb of a pharaoh I knew little about. And yet, I asked permission of our Egyptian tour guide to do just that.

As I made my way up the steep mountain range lined with armed guards on camelback along its rim, I watched as two of my traveling companions, Laurie and Carlo Tonon from Sudbury, Ontario Canada, made their way to the outskirts far beyond the resting place of Thutmosis IV.

Before long, Laurie, a fourth-degree black belt and Carlo, a sixth-degree black belt and martial arts sensei were out of my sight.

Nearing the entrance to my destination, I was greeted by a friendly group of Italian travelers, who warned me that the descent into Thutmosis IV tomb was steep and trying. Wearing smiles of satisfaction upon their faces, members of the group assured me that I would enjoy the glorious hieroglyphics and the exquisite sarcophagus that awaited my arrival.

It was kind of them to warn me about the difficulties of maneuvering the tomb's interior terrain. Had they known, I am certain that they would have warned me about the life-altering experience that was waiting for me as well.

Expecting to encounter a similar size group of travelers waiting to enter the crypt, I was surprised to find that I was the only person wishing to enter the pharaoh's grave. Handing my entry voucher to the assigned ticket taker, I was invited to step foot onto the descending platform which would lead me down a vertical incline deep into the heart of the burial chamber of the Dreamer.

With caution and very aware of my footing, I began the downward journey into the dimly lit cavern. The colorful Egyptian hieroglyphs that adorned both sides of the narrow, stone-hewed corridor were, in some cases, still brilliantly clear and vibrant. The energy that surrounded me was both sacred and exciting. It was everything I had hoped to experience and soon I would realize, far more than I thought it would be.

With approximately one third of the downward climb behind me, I became aware of a hieroglyph I had not yet seen painted on any of the other temple antiquities. Directly to the right of me was a large multihued bumble bee - a sign that would prove to be a portent of imminent danger.

Turning my gaze from the hieroglyphic harbinger hanging just above my shoulder, I focused once again on the steep downhill incline that was before me. Within a matter of seconds I could feel the presence of someone approaching me from behind. It was a physical presence that I was sensing and one that was determined to reach me in little to no time. A nudge to the upper portion of my back proved what my senses had been telling me, someone was on my heels and in a hurry to help me down the remainder of the platform steps.

Taking me by the arm, I was now being led downward by a man I did not know. His tall, gangly frame towered over my own. For a split second, I was rattled by fear.

In another instant, I heard my guardian Angel speak to me; "Dana, the ordeal that you now find yourself in is simply a test. The one who wishes to speak of and teach about the Angelic with authenticity, must experience the power and resourcefulness of the Angels firsthand."

Simultaneously, my call for assistance to the Holy Mother and to the Archangel St. Michael was already leaving the silence of my heart and mind; "Holy Mother, Michael, Archangel of the 7th Heavenly Realm, I am calling to you. Please help me to see clearly what is going on here. Guide me in my words and decisions. Thank you for sending help to me!"

In what seemed like an eternity, but in reality was only a matter of minutes, my antagonist and I had reached the bottom of the Dreamer's tomb. In front of a sarcophagus dripping in the painted energy of the Mother Goddess Isis, we stood face to face.

Remembering what the Angels had moments before told me and staring directly into his onyx colored, almost lifeless eyes, I was the first to speak. "If you are an Angel of darkness who has come to challenge the veracity of my Light, you will not win. If you are an Angel of Light who has come to help me realize the fullness of my Light within, I am grateful."

Jerking me by the wrist, my adversary pulled me around and to the back of Thutmosis' antediluvian sarcophagus. With perhaps 3 feet of space between the massive granite coffin and the wall of the tomb, we were thrust together in what felt like a crypt of our own.

There was some part of me that felt great pity for the young man who had tightened his grip upon my arms. I couldn't help but wonder if he was a willing partner to this bit of mayhem, or someone who had been caught up on the spirit of something he knew little of.

"I know that you truly don't want to hurt me, do you?" I asked.

A few words in his native tongue fell from his lips as a miracle began to unfold just outside the entrance to the tomb.

The sounds of people rushing down the length of the stairs leading to Thutmosis' final resting place came closer. Frantic shouts in English and the sounds of the Egyptian ticket taker sounding a warning to my nemesis in Arabic, filled the descending corridor as my challenger once again grabbed me by the wrist in order to pull me away from the wall of the burial chamber and back out in front of the fully winged Isis.

Through a gentle mist of dust, I could see the faces of my Canadian friends, Laurie and Carlo. Without missing a beat or catching a breath, Carlo commanded both men to step away.

As Laurie stood in stunned silence, Carlo reached for my hand and boomed, "She is coming with us! Do you understand this?"

Both men nodded in the affirmative as Carlo and Laurie ushered me to the top of the tomb and out into the brilliant Egyptian sunlight.

Without looking back, the three of us made our way back down the side of the sandy foothill, until at last we came to a resting spot near the base of the Valley of the Kings.

Clearly upset and with much concern for my safety, Carlo spoke in the most restrained manner he could muster, "My God, Denise, do you know what that man intended to do to you? Do you have any idea his intentions? That man wanted to end your life! Do you realize that? What in heaven's name were you doing there alone?"

My Angel team had obviously not spoken to Carlo's Angel team. Or, if they had, Carlo didn't get the message that the previous exercise in Angelic intervention had been just that; an exercise.

"It was just a test." That was my response. "A test? What kind of a test are you talking about, Denise? That's one helluva test, my friend!"

Laurie and Carlo waited for my answer.

"Sometimes, life sends some pretty profound experiences to test us mere mortals. Trials by fire help us to understand the power of the Light and the power of that same Light that lives within us. The Light always wins. Today was another reminder of that unchanging fact."

Trying to lighten up the atmosphere, I continued, "When I knew that I was in trouble, I called out to the Archangel St. Michael and his legions of Light for help. And look, they sent the Canadian Mounties to my rescue!"

Not knowing whether to laugh or cry, both shook their heads in disbelief.

"How did you manage to find me?" I asked.

"We were clear on the other end of the valley, Laurie explained, when I sensed an urgency to leave the tomb that we were visiting. Without really knowing why, I told Carlo I wanted to visit the burial place of Thutmosis IV and he agreed. The closer we got to the entrance of the tomb, I could feel that something wasn't right. When we got right up to the door, one of the gentlemen at the entrance ran right past us, and began shouting as he made his way down the stairs. Carlo and I knew something was very wrong, so we followed him down into the crypt. We couldn't believe our eyes when we saw that young man pull you out to the front of the sarcophagus. I knew right then, why I had been feeling the way I had been. Thank goodness you're okay!"

Without further conversation, we made our way back to our traveling party. Each of us trying to digest the events that had just taken place, we spoke very little as the tour bus finally approached the waiting area.

Finding our seats within the safe confines of our motor coach, Carlo was the last one to enter. Without warning and with great exasperation, he exclaimed out loud, "I have never seen such tomfoolery in all my life!"

Stunned, I turned to look at him just as Laurie was replying, "Carlo, what did you just say?"

"I said," Carlo declared, "that I have never seen such tomfoolery in all of my life as I saw today in the Valley of the Kings!"

Laurie countered, "Carlo, where did you hear that word? I've never heard you use it before."

"Now that you mentioned it," he replied, "I really don't know. It just kind of flew out of my mouth. All I do know is that a glass of wine is in order tonight … maybe two!"

Earlier, I was convinced that Carlo's Angels hadn't clued him in to the events that were to unfold. In that instant, however, I knew that on some level, the message had indeed been received loud and clear.

The three of us spoke to very few people about what happened that day in the Valley of the Kings. To me, it was a profound lesson in the reality of Angelic intervention and the mighty bond of love that exists between those who inhabit the realm of heaven and the human beings that occupy earth.

It did, after all, send a couple of Canada's finest, dressed as black belt martial artists with a heart of gold; a pair of Light warriors who would become my lifetime friends.

Traveling to ancient Egypt has become a part of my life that I greatly enjoy. From her beautiful people and exotic terrain, to the prehistoric antiquities and relics of faith, it is a country and a people who are rich in history, love, and so much joy.

Emancipation

A soul's journey toward spiritual, emotional, mental and physical emancipation is one that is fraught with life altering dangers. The danger of losing old belief systems, lifetime friends, family members and colleagues is very real and for many, a tangible blockade to the gateway of freedom.

Slavery to the illusions that we are taught to buy into as children is often our first step on the road to self-imposed bondage. By the time we reach our teenage years, we are already held captive to society's ideas of beauty, personal appeal and power. Add to that a concoction of unreal expectations, a heavy dose of religious and familial guilt, and the chains of suppression are locked securely around our mind, our hearts and our life as we enter adulthood.

I believe, that into the life of each person, comes the day when our spirit cries out for freedom. It is a wail and call from deep within us that rises up to declare independence from our endless servitude to the fears that keeps us from our joy, our self-realization and most importantly, the avocation of our Soul. It is that day of reckoning that brings us to our knees and either keeps us there, or propels us to become our own Harriet Tubman, armed and ready to set the captive free.

What of the slave holder? The master who holds our freedom in their greedy grip? What right do they have to our joy, our sense of peace, our love and our spiritual fulfillment on earth? They have only the rights that we have assigned to them. Rights that we have authority to rescind at any time.

During my emancipation process, which has been decades in the doing, all of those fears that I harbored about change, abandonment, shaming, anger and loss came to me with every shackle that I unlocked. Yet, each time I stepped further into freedom, the air around me became more breathable. My ability to truly see *who* and *what* had imprisoned so much of my joy came into clear focus. The truth of the matter is that one of my own worst adversaries was *me*. My inability to love myself enough to live a life that I loved, had also become my jailer.

My quest for freedom finds my definition of family and friends permanently and beautifully altered. My slavery to guilt, shame and abandonment are a thing of past; going away with those who wished to hold me captive to them. In their stead, I am joined by souls who wish to share, to explore, to grow with and love me in my unfettered bareness.

I bless those masters and jailers that once were, for what they have taught me about loving myself and living this gift of life that Creator so graciously gave me, to the fullness of my being. Their lessons have served me well; I am free.

Sacred Wisdom

"Sacred wisdom is not given.

It is earned by the soul that is ready

to wield it in a positive,

loving manner.

We are, after all,

responsible for the knowledge

that we acquire and the way

in which we use it."

-Denise Iwaniw-Francisco

What of Prayer?

Sending loving thoughts; keeping a Gratitude Journal; reciting the rosary; mindful meditation; lovingly sewing a button on a shirt - all of these are a form of prayer.

Each one of them is far more powerful than we could ever imagine. Like raindrops to a thirsty flower, prayer fills us with loving energy and rejuvenates our Spirit. And, like a raindrop falling on a still pond, its healing effects ripple outward infinitely.

At times when we feel we have nothing to offer someone in the way of comfort, we often ask, "What can I do to help?" The answer sounds so simple and yet I believe that it is *the* most powerful source *and* force of comfort and healing in the Universe. The answer is: "Prayer."

Monument outside Rosslyn Chapel, Scotland, 2012

Prayer comes from one of the most mighty energy centers in the Universe; the heart. When a thought or gesture is done from the heart, it sends forward an immensely powerful intention that is surrounded with love. One single person sending a prayer to the Creator on behalf of themselves or others creates a shift of such magnitude we cannot begin to conceive of it. Even when our prayers are not answered in exactly the same manner we had intended, we can be assured that they will indeed be answered in a way that will serve our greatest and highest good.

Recently, medical studies have tested the recovery period for those being prayed for. The overwhelming results have been speedier recovery times and in some cases recoveries that are nothing short of a miracle.

The healing energy of a prayer is first received in our heart center. Its loving intention fills us with love and Light. From there it radiates outward to our entire aura, balancing our energy centers and lifting us up spiritually and physically. We radiate in the Spirit, when we are full of love. When we radiate love, we attract love in return.

Many times when I am in session with a client, I receive a message from a loved one on the other side that the prayers that have been sent to them have been heard and received, but more than that, the prayers have been "felt." On more than one occasion, it has been described to me as a "warm, blue energy" that feels like an embrace; it has even been described to me as a warm fuzzy sweater. Just as prayer has an uplifting effect on those of us on the physical plane, so too does it have an uplifting effect on those in Spirit.

Whether it is one solitary voice, or the voices of a multitude, prayer is a means by which change can be affected locally and globally. So, while you are at home visualizing the entire world basking in a healing pink embrace, rest assured that your healing prayer is indeed being felt in places you've never dreamed of going and by people you may never meet...in this lifetime anyway.

Ganesha Altar, Kaduval Temple, Kauai, 2017

Prayers for Mní Wičhóni– Sacred and Life Giving Waters

Očeti Šakówiŋ Othí at Standing Rock Reservation

"Sister, I need you to come up here to Standing Rock to help me pray."

So began a conversation with my adopted 'thibló' or older brother, Guy Dullknife.

My brother, a Lakota Sioux elder, founding member of the American Indian Movement, Vietnam veteran and father of more than a dozen children had been named as the Director of the Očeti Šakówiŋ Camp. This camp would become known around the world and start a movement around Unci Maka, 'Grandmother Earth, like no other.

Očeti Šakówiŋ means, Seven Fires Council of the Great Sioux Nation. Each one of those Seven Councils had one 'wičháša wakȟáŋ', holy man living at that camp to provide spiritual insight and direction to those living at the camp. Those seven holy men asked Guy to lead the camp and with a humble heart, he agreed.

Days earlier I had been made aware of a call by Chief Arvol Looking Horse that went out to all sacred pipe carriers and spiritual leaders to come to Standing Rock Reservation to assist with the peaceful protest of protection for the sacred waters, which were being threatened by the construction of a massive oil pipeline being laid through sacred, unceded tribal lands. In other words, the pipeline was going straight through tribal lands that were taken by the federal government, without consent of the tribal nation. Should the pipeline leak or break, the pollution threatened to poison the largest clean water supply to the tribal nation and the largest aquifer in the central United States.

Oceti Sakowin Camp, Standing Rock, North Dakota 2016

Additionally, the pipeline trenches were unceremoniously and quite cruelly, unearthing ancient burial grounds containing the relics of the beloved ancestors.

Thus began the worldwide movement to defend and protect the sacred water of Grandmother Earth. Mní Wíčhóni! (In the Lakota Sioux language, Mní Wičhóni means, "Water is Life").

Each morning at 4:30 a.m., Guy would rap his carved, wooden walking stick on the side of my tent to awaken me and my hunka, 'adopted' sister, Neshi from our sleep. Both of us would climb out of our sleeping bags, roll off of our cots and quickly dress by flashlight in the frigid North Dakota morning temperatures.

In the dark, with only the Morning Star Woman to guide us, the three of us would slowly make our way to the central ceremonial fire to begin the morning prayers for the nearly ten thousand people who were yet asleep in their tents and tipis.

Guy and me

As was the case each and every morning, the sacred fire keeper greeted us with a soft, "Good morning" and a warm offer of a hot cup of coffee. And after offering a bit of tobacco into the fire, and saying our morning prayers of gratitude, we took a seat around the fire and waited for the microphone and speaker system to be prepared for Guy.

Without fanfare and at exactly 5:00 a.m., Guy would walk us over to the microphone to begin forming a prayer circle and to awaken every sleeping soul at Očeti Šakówiŋ Camp.

With oil pipeline crews working around the clock to the east of us and under a canopy of brilliant stars in the indigo pre-dawn sky, "Kiktá po! Wake up!" were the first words spoken in Lakota and English and broadcast clear across the camp.

"It's time to get up! It's time to start the day! Kiktá po! Wake up!"

Gradually, water protectors made their way to the central fire, the prayer circle and to a time of deep ceremony to honor the sacred spirit of water.

As 'Áŋpaó Wičháȟpi', Morning Star Woman, rose higher into the sky and the birth of the amber colored sun could be seen beyond the grassy hills on the Cannonball River, people from all four corners of Grandmother Earth gathered in an enormous circle to hear Guy sing ancient Lakota prayer songs and to offer words of wisdom and encouragement to those gathered. The first prayer song was always to the 'Waŋŋblí Gleška Oyáte', the Spotted Eagle Nation, asking for guidance to walk each step of our lives with a good heart.

After the prayer songs, Guy would hand the microphone over to me to lead the group in prayers of gratitude for the gift of a brand new day and an opportunity to work with our global brothers and sisters to make the world a more loving place for all. Neshi, would then offer words of encouragement to the hundreds gathered around the ceremonial fire.

"Love one another. Be good to one another. If you see someone struggling, offer them a hand. If someone can't speak the English language, try to help them understand what is being said, or learn words in *their* language. We are all in this together. Pray for those who are working on the pipeline. They are our relatives, too. We must work together to protect the sacred waters and *all* life on Grandmother Earth. Mitákuye oyáš'iŋ, 'we are all related'." Those were the closing words that my brother Guy shared with everyone who gathered each day.

Finally, at the end of morning prayers and prayer songs, a ceremony to honor mni wiconi the 'sacred waters', would be led by a group of women from the Navajo Nation. Water that had been prayed over would be offered to each person in circle, as more prayer songs were sung and ultimately, a ceremonial walk to the Cannonball River would take place, and offerings of prayer and tobacco would be given to the sacred spirit of water.

In the evening, along with my nieces and nephews, we gathered around our small family campfire to retell the stories of our day at Camp, frequently speaking of the importance of prayer, not only to begin the day in the right way but to see us through the trials and triumphs of every day.

During our short stay at Očeti Šakówíŋ Camp, I watched as lives, including mine, were forever changed. Hope was inspired, and a sense of higher purpose was gained, through positive prayers, encouraging words and the sharing of ancestral stories and songs. Although the pipeline was eventually completed, something far greater was accomplished by the prayers and prayerful people at Standing Rock. A current of change flowed out of Oceti Sakowin, traveling across and around all of Grandmother Earth, raising the awareness of our relationship to Mother Nature, to one another and to all things that are seen *and* unseen.

The spirit of mitákuye oyáš'iŋ was reborn on earth, just as 'Ptesáŋwiŋ', the White Buffalo Calf Woman had foretold.

About My Moccasins, Our Star Ancestors and the Lakota Star Quilt

As they were being placed on my feet for the very first time, my elder sister, Dellmarie Dullknife-Bradfield explained, "These single, dark blue beads that I placed on the leggings of your moccasins represent your relationship with our star nation relatives."

It was my older sister herself who had lovingly and painstakingly created my beautiful, knee high, moccasins. Each of the thousands of tiny blue, silver, and white beads had been hand stitched upon them with a prayer; a prayer for me.

Dellmarie placing the moccasins on my feet

The Moccasin Ceremony represents the welcoming of a new relative into a 'thiyóšpayé' or family and indicates a commitment to walk the 'Čhaŋkú Lúta', Red Road alongside one another. It is a ceremony deep in spirituality.

My Indian name, Wakiŋyaŋ Tȟo, Blue Thunder, comes to me from my soul's home in the big bear, the star constellation known as Ursa Major. A long, long time ago, the blue star located in the middle of the dipper could be seen with the physical eye. It is known as the cosmic home to seers and spirit doulas.

Earlier that same day at my sister Barb's home on the Pine Ridge Indian Reservation in South Dakota, I listened as my čhuwć' Dellmarie shared the story of the Lakota Star Quilt, as it was told to her.

"A long time ago, it was the custom of our People to gift buffalo hide robes as a way to honor someone. At that time, those buffalo hide blankets kept the People warm. Then, as the buffalo were all killed off by the U.S. military and immigrants, Native women had to begin making blankets from the fabric they purchased from the pioneers who had come West."

Everyone in the room listened intently as Dellmarie continued. "The way the story of the Star Quilt was told to me was that many years ago, a Lakota woman became very ill. In her feverish dreams she was given a message from a star nations relative who lives in our ancient home on the northern star, Polaris. In her dream the Lakota woman was told to have her young daughter sew a colorful quilt with a large Northern Star quilted right in the middle of it. Once the star quilt was finished, she was then to wrap herself up in the quilted blanket and allow her star relatives to help heal her. Her daughter did as she was asked, hand sewing the very first Lakota Star Quilt with the Northern Star placed perfectly in the center of it. When it was completed, she wrapped her mother in the blanket and together they prayed for the healing of her mother's illness. Within days, the woman was completely healed and the legend of the Lakota Star Quilt was born."

Lakota Star Quilt with White Buffalo in the Center

UFOs and Star People

As a youth in the 1970s, my fascination with unidentified flying objects and extraterrestrial beings was fueled by B-rated movies, tabloid magazines and grainy, black and white documentaries on television. It wasn't until I grew older and began having meaningful conversations about the existence of UFOs with friends and colleagues that my thirst for a first-hand experience would grow to become something of a spiritual quest.

One conversation in particular, really spurred my interest.

While enjoying morning coffee on the deck of a Nile River cruise boat in Egypt, a good friend of mine and a former airline pilot confided in me, that on more than one occasion, while captaining a commercial Boeing 747, she had encountered UFOs. She also shared with me the fear and surprise on the faces of inexperienced co-pilots who encountered the large space ships for the very first time, while in her presence.

While her experiences were very real, they were not to be discussed with her passengers, co-workers, or, for that matter, ever - at all.

According to my friend and other pilots who have come forth to share their UFO encounters publicly, there is an apparent 'code of silence' amongst commercial pilots and an unspoken 'don't ask, don't tell' policy at government agencies.

I felt blessed that my friend shared her numerous experiences with me. Looking back, I now know that they were preparing me for my first encounter of the galactic kind.

It was dusk on the Pine Ridge Indian Reservation in South Dakota and I was sitting around a sacred ceremonial fire with several others who were also waiting to enter an evening sweat lodge. Sitting next to me was the holy man who would lead the ceremony. He was also my teacher.

Leaning in closer to him, I asked, "What do the Lakota elders teach us about unidentified flying objects and extraterrestrials?"

Chuckling, he answered, "First of all, we identified them a long time ago. Our star ancestors are not unidentified to us, and their star ships are very real."

"Will I ever see one?" I asked.

"When you are ready to see a star ship and to meet a star relative, you will."

That was his short response and the end of our conversation about UFOs and extraterrestrial beings.

Fast forward six Earth months and a blink of the Cosmic Eye later…

Back in Michigan and driving home from an evening event in the city, I found myself taking my usual passage through the busy suburbs. Streets that were typically quite hectic were unusually quiet that night.

Motoring by my favorite grocery store, I saw an incredibly bright light that was moving very quickly in the darkened sky above me and to my left. To my horror, the bright light appeared to be falling to Earth. Convinced that I was seeing a large airliner that was plunging from the sky and preparing to crash around me, I pulled my car off to the side of the unusually empty thoroughfare to reach into my purse and retrieve my cell phone.

Keeping one eye on the light that was growing larger while hurtling toward Earth, and fumbling around for my phone to call for emergency assistance, I was stunned by what happened next.

Without a sound, the whooshing of treetops or a sweeping wind, the descending light, that I gauged to be approximately the size of a football field, came to a complete and utter stop, resting just above the trees that were located across the street from my parked car.

Silently suspended in the inky blue sky above me was a brightly lit, perfectly round, star ship.

Breathless and frozen in place and time, I watched the craft. I felt as though it was watching me, too.

Within moments and without warning, the flying object flew straight upward and quickly disappeared from my sight.

Gathering my wits about me, I reminded myself to take a deep breath and exhale. In the next moment, I heard a gentle, discarnate voice say to me, "Blue Thunder Woman, you were ready to see us and to know that we are real. There will be more visitations in the years to come."

Still sitting in the driver's seat of my stationary vehicle. I took a few more deep breaths and offered an audible, "Thank you!" to whomever it was that had graced me with the experience of seeing a star ship and meeting the star people in such an obvious way.

A couple of years later, I was invited to a metaphysical conference in Asheville, North Carolina, to present a lecture to several hundred people about the importance of exploring, refining and sharing our spiritual gifts and talents. The morning of my presentation, I was awakened just after dawn by the presence of what I can best describe as an electric green being that was standing next to the right side of my bed. Approximately 6 feet tall, it seemed to be observing me. Its energy was pulsating and palpable.

At first, I was startled and a bit frightened by the company of this slender, green creature. Simultaneously, I was joyful to be in the company of a relative from the stars. Without exchanging words, we simply looked at one another for what felt like 30 seconds, and the star-being faded from view.

With the holy man's words once again ringing in my mind, I gave thanks for this interaction and joyfully await my next encounter with a star ancestor.

Spiritual Gifts

"What you are talking about, Catherine Therese, are the gifts of the spirit,

expressions of the charismata." - Father Keller

I was 15 years old and living in the state of Minnesota. Like other 15 year-old Catholic boys and girls who attended my parish church, I was preparing to undergo the rite of Catholic Confirmation.

In preparation for this blessed sacrament, each of us was instructed by our catechism teacher to choose a confirmation name, the name of a saint that we were particularly fond of, and one that we wished to emulate in our lives.

For me that was easy. I chose the name Catherine, after St. Catherine of Siena. Born in Siena, Italy on March 25, 1347, Catherine was a church mystic, a seer, prolific writer, philosopher, and theologian. A member of the Dominican order, she was a woman of substance who often found herself embroiled in the politics of the day. Catherine balanced her earthly life and her heavenly life by spending a great deal of her time, deep in prayer and meditation. This bold, transcendent woman is the patron saint of the United States, Europe and Italy.

Although I preferred the likes of the mystical St. Teresa of Avila, my parents also wanted me to choose the name, Therese, after the 19th century French, Carmelite saint, Therese of Lisieux. Also known as the Little Flower of Jesus, Therese of Lisieux was a humble poet, playwright, mystic and a self-described apostle of the apostles. Her physical life ended at the age of 24 after a long and painful battle with tuberculosis. Pope Pius X referred to her as the greatest saint of the modern age.

Hence my Catholic confirmation name, Catherine Therese.

Following the naming mass, attended by myself and my catechism classmates there was to be a big celebration in the parish hall. My fellow confirmands made their way directly to the party, while I waited alone in the front pew of the now dimly lit church, waiting for our parish priest to finish tidying up the altar.

Noticing that he was not alone, the robed priest left his altar duties and walked up to where I was seated. With a gentle smile on his face, betraying his normally stern demeanor, he asked me why I was not at the party with my friends in the church hall. I explained to Father that I had questions about myself, that I felt he could answer.

"Father, how is it that I can see people who are supposed to be dead? Why can I see what I believe are angels and other sorts of spirits? I've been able to see and hear them since I was a little girl and no one has been able to explain it to me."

In a very calm voice and gently touching my right shoulder, the Catholic priest offered these words, "What you are talking about, Catherine Therese, are the gifts of the spirit, expressions of the charismata. These spiritual abilities are very real and what you are describing to me are examples of charismatic gifts. Earlier this week, he continued, I participated in the ritual of exorcism here in the city. Not all spirits are good spirits, Catherine Therese. You must remember this. What you have been given are gifts from God, but what also comes with the mystical gifts is *great* responsibility. One day you will fully understand what I am talking about. For now, try to be a regular teenager and go have some fun with your classmates. Soon enough, you will meet people who will be able to help you grow in the gifts of the spirit."

With that, he gave me a gentle hug and shooed me out of the church and into the celebration hall.

A sense of relief flooded me, following my talk with Father. While I didn't have all of the details, at least I hadn't been ridiculed or accused of having a fanciful imagination. Off to the confirmation festivities I went, knowing that someone in my life understood me.

Some fifteen years later … my teachers and the mystical teachings would begin to filter into my life and my work as an author and spiritual teacher would ensue. The avocation of my soul began to evolve and the path that it brought with it, continues unfold before me.

The Greatest Teachers

"The greatest teachers

walk through the greatest fires

in order to teach with *integrity*

and authenticity."

-Denise Iwaniw-Francisco

My Philosophy of Light

Promptly upon my ordination as a minister in 2008, a young boy about seven years of age walked up to me at a social gathering and asked, "Miss Denise, what is God? I mean, who is God *really*?"

Thus began an enchanting conversation about what multitudes of children intrinsically know about their origin, but that the journey of a human lifetime often strips away from them.

"To me, I responded, God is love. Plain and simple. God is the Light of Love."

With a clap of his young hands and a hug around my waist, Logan delightfully responded, "Me too!" and off he ran to play with the other children.

A punishing, vengeful God is not the God that I grew up with. Neither at home nor during my many years in Catholic catechism classes was I ever presented with the idea that some mean, bearded old man floating around on a heavenly cloud with a willow switch in hand was just waiting to reprimand me.

Trust me, there was a whole lot of discipline in our very military, Catholic household, but none of it ever came from God or the heavenly angels or any of the holy, ascended saints.

Even as a young girl, I was widely aware of the presence of Light in the world. Albeit a world that very few others could see. There has always been what I call a 'softness' of Light that accompanies me on my journey. I believe it guides us all. It comes with the presence of those whom I have loved, who have travelled home to Creator and now wear their spiritual vestments of Light, the raiment of their soul. When they visit me in my waking time or sleeping time, this exquisite, ethereal Light shines around them and *through* them. It feels like love.

The realization of the presence of angels, a blessing that I received since the moment of my birth, has given to me the understanding that angels *do* appear in many forms and often, when we are least expecting them.

Often, I am asked how one knows when they've *truly* been visited by an angel. In return I typically ask the person to describe how they *felt* in the presence of the being(s) that they are questioning me about.

Whether describing the presence of a Light that suddenly bathed a room in its brilliance; the presence of a discernible, kindly being with or without spectacular wings; the sudden appearance of an animal persistent in its wanting to be seen; or a *knowing* that one is simply not alone; a thread common to all of these angelic visitations is an indescribable feeling of love and most often … the presence of an unearthly Light.

Years ago, I had the opportunity to understand this love and this Light in a very personal way. Lying in a hospital bed, after having suffered a left brain stroke, I found myself hearing the otherworldly voice of the Archangel St. Michael telling me that I could come Home; that my work here on earth was complete. He explained that I had a choice to stay and work further on earth, or that I could also choose to come rest.

Alone in my darkened hospital room and briefly leaving my body on the current of his voice, I saw myself in that medical bed, very ill and yet shrouded in an effervescent, glowing Light. The Light dimmed around my physical body, as my spiritual body seemingly gained in strength. Both bodies, physical and spiritual, were bound by a stream of Light that seemed to feed both, based on need. At that moment, I knew beyond all knowing, that this Light was love. Not the kind we describe in our human relationships. This love is vast. It is cosmic. It is intelligent. I believe it is the sum total of all of thoughts that Creator thinks and all that Creator continually creates out of its infinite sea of love.

An avid student of philosophy and arcane mystery school teachings, my human experience with the Light that evening in the hospital, to me, proved that what the ancient philosophers of Light had always pondered, sang and written about. With my life now richer in this knowledge, I chose to stay here on earth.

The great alchemists teach us that everything that we perceive outside of ourselves is also contained within us. Teachers of the arcane wisdom take it a step further to reveal that even the Light of the angels that we beckon *to* us, are simultaneously called from *within* us to create a cosmic, alchemical reaction. By whatever name we call out to them, we are summoning that same angelic stardust contained inside us. Once met, we find ourselves in the presence of heavenly beings of Love and Light.

My philosophy of Light is simple. I believe that we *are* the Light and Love of the angels, the saints, the sinners and wise poets. We are Mother Nature, Father Sun, the stars and moons. We are God in expression and the hands of the angels on earth who came here to play, to dance, to love, to learn, to inform, to ascend and to shine.

Together, now more than ever, it is important for each and every one of us to shine our Love Light here on earth.

Haŋbléčheyapi: Vision Quest

When I awoke this morning, I was greeted by the booming sound of the 'Wakíŋyaŋ Oyaté'; the Thunder Nation. Their voices calling me to my 'čhaŋnúŋpa wakȟáŋ', my sacred prayer pipe and to a time of meditation and conversation with Spirit.

My altar, gently lit by a single candle, and the orange embers of burning sage, I heard them speak to me in their crackly, lightning voices that are so forcefully pristine. Within the smoke that billowed upward from my čhaŋnúŋpa wakȟáŋ', their faces became clear.

"Wakíŋyaŋ Tȟó Wíŋyaŋ ... Blue Thunder Woman; write about what we told you while you were put up on the hill. Remember what we told you about the heavens on earth? Write about that one. Do that."

And so, I shall...

The Lakota Sioux elders told me that when I came down from that hill, I would never be the same woman I once was; they were right.

The Crying for a Dream ceremony is truthful. During this sacred rite, a person is gifted with an insight as to why they chose to come to earth and what dream they came here to fulfill. The Ancestors and Spirits visit them and tell them honest, ancient things about themselves and Creation.

Before going up on the hill; as the elders call it, I was placed in several consecutive sweat lodges for purification and prayers for clear visions and strength. Then I waited in silence for the time to be just right for the ascent to my hilltop vision quest altar.

Out of the silence came the excited voice of the ceremonial fire keeper, Melvin High Hawk. "Blue Thunder Woman, the thunderers are ready for you now!"

With his right arm raised toward the direction of the West, he continued, "Wakíŋyaŋ Tȟó Wíŋyaŋ, *see*, the Relatives are waiting for you. Get your čhaŋnúŋpa wakȟáŋ and your prayer ties, it's time. To the west, a giant, bright white thunder cloud covered the vastness of the blue, mid-day sky. I could see the internal movement of that enormous being from where I stood. I was being called to ceremony.

Alone, with my pipe and a single grandma spider, *'iktómi'*, who never left my side, I was soon sitting within my sacred altar of 404 prayer ties, while Melvin tended the fire far below. Both of us remained in our portion of the ceremony until the Holy Man said it was time for me to come back, purify myself again and tell him about my 'dream'.

It was during the deep of night, with a canopy of stars directly overhead that I heard yet another group of ancestral voices speak to me rapid fire and in unison.

"Wakíŋyaŋ Tȟó Wíŋyaŋ, 'Blue Thunder Woman' remember what we are going to say now. Remember this. Human beings are waiting for heaven to come to earth. Tell them, Blue Thunder Woman, that **they are** the heavens on earth. They need to wake up and remember this! Every time a human being shines their love on Earth, they bring heaven to earth. Tell them this. Do you understand us?"

"Hiyé. Yes, I understand you." I replied.

The Spirits implored further, "Remember to laugh. Laughter is good! Tell them this, Wakíŋyaŋ Tȟó Wíŋyaŋ. Laughter brings the good spirits close to them."

In the years since my life changing experience on the hill, I have done as the Spirits and Ancestors asked. I've shared that story with family and friends, clients and students, in university lecture halls, classes at The Temple Within School of Sacred Studies, and now with you, my dear readers.

The extraordinary experience of a human lifetime is a profound gift that our soul gets to experience for a very short while. I believe that we have come here to be the eyes, ears, hands and heart of the Maker in motion; the Creator made manifest to express its' Light and Love upon the earthly plane of existence. We came here to joyfully, courageously shine our own unique light on Grandmother Earth and in doing so, bring the matrix of heavenly love into deep reality right here, right now.

The time of the return of the White Buffalo Calf Woman is now. Sitting on the proverbial fence is no longer allowed by the Universe. Stand up! Speak out! Volunteer! Lend a hand, share, shine, and don't forget to laugh along the way!

You are, after all, a manifestation of heaven on Earth.

Wolf: Spirit of the Guardian and Teacher

Wolf 'Suŋgmanitu Tȟaŋka' – Lakota Sioux

Medicine: Guardian and Teacher

Star Nations Correspondence: Lupus Constellation

I am the protector of all of the Great Spirit's children; young and old.

Through the four seasons of the sacred hoop of life, the newness of spring, the heat of summer, the harvest of autumn, and bitterness of winter, I walk with the medicine of the elders.

I am the guardian and teacher of the ancient wisdom and companion of those who hold the integrity of the Old Ways.

Walk the good Red Road with me, child, and listen as I teach you about the Great Mysteries and what the old ones have always known. I will tell you the secrets of the winds, the moons, the sun, and stars and you will learn the truth of who you are.

Daily Mantra:

"My life is my legacy. I teach the children well."

-from the Animal Totems Empowerment Deck,

by Denise Iwaniw-Francisco

My love affair with the spirit of the wolf started as a young child. Her blue and piercing, all knowing eyes, an impervious air of strength and protection, as well as an all-encompassing feeling of loyalty and love, are my earliest remembrances of my Spirit wolf.

My family and friends could not see her, but as for me, she was as real as any of them and quite frankly, seemed to know me, my fears and my needs far better than they did. I named her Sheba.

Many children grow up with 'imaginary friends' that are in fact very real companions who reside in the non-physical world. Often times these invisible buddies appear to look like other human children and at other times, they are reported to look like angels. Every so often however, a child may convey that their unseen friends are actually animals. I was blessed to enjoy the hidden fellowship of all of the above; children, angels *and* animals alike.

At the age of 17 I received a very special gift from my dad, my very own real life Sheba, a purebred Siberian husky dog that was the embodiment of my Spirit wolf. For the time that she remained on this earth plane with me, Sheba and I were inseparable. It wasn't until she had an encounter with a rabid animal that our earthly relationship ended.

Heartbroken at the loss of my wolf, Sheba, even my understanding of reincarnation and animal spirit allies could not comfort me. Then, one evening not long after her passing, she came to my bedroom in her Spirit body once more. In that one instant, I understood that her incarnation into physicality, however short, had been a rare and precious gift. I also knew, that I would never again be without her.

Always the protector and teacher, helping me to see with different eyes, Sheba has been at my side during glorious times as well as times in my life when I've felt vulnerable to darkness. She is present throughout sacred ceremonies such as my 'haŋbléčheyapi' or vision quest, during my inípi ceremonies, the making of the relatives' ceremonies and ministerial ordination. Regal in her gray and silver fur, others with second sight also see her and feel her loving, protective stance.

Our four legged brothers and sisters are far more than just animals. They, like us, are the living expression of Creator; each unique in their own personality, spirit, nature and gifts. Like their human relatives, they are loved beyond all earthly understanding by the One who creates *all* things. We are after all, all related.

My work as a seer gives me beautiful opportunities to teach clients and students that not only do animals make wonderful family pets, they are also incredibly gifted spirit guides and teachers.

Like humans, the animal kingdom is also a divine expression of Creator's love on earth. After physical life is complete, animals also experience a joyful return to Home, their original state of grace. The deep affection that we can have for animals creates bonds of love that survive physical incarnations and lifetimes.

I've met with many a human being who has expressed horror at the thought that their beloved pet is a soulless being. Sadly, this is a teaching that has been perpetuated by the ignorance of *some* religious belief systems. Not only is that not the case, our animal brothers and sisters are actually divine messengers from the realms of Spirit, some of whom actually incarnate and occupy a place in our homes and our hearts in any given lifetime.

Time and again, when meeting with clients who come to see me for spiritual guidance, I am given the great blessing to deliver messages from their beloved family members who, in their lifetime, sported fur, feathers, scales, hair, and fins. I am also honored to introduce clients and students to spirit guides who send animal spirits as messengers from the Divine.

It's All a Numbers Game

"Why didn't they teach us about Buddha, Mohammed, Krishna, Wakȟáŋ Tȟáŋka, Shiva, Shakti, or Kuan Yin in any of my catechism classes?" I asked my Catholic spiritual director.

"Because," she said, "It's all a numbers game. If you liked one of them more than you like Jesus, you might take your religious business elsewhere."

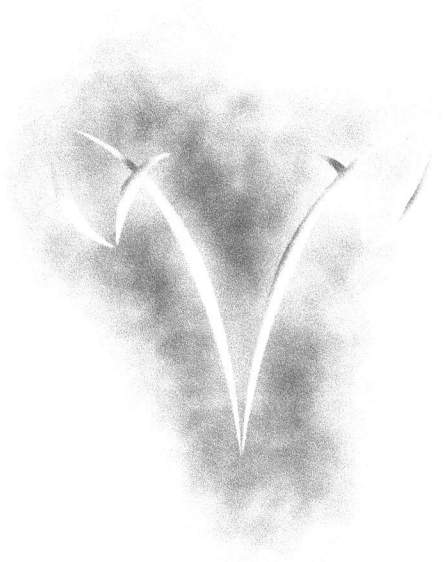

Satguru, Kaduval Temple, Kauai 2017

The Dark Night and the Light of a New Day

"When you find yourself dancing with the Dark Knight, rest in the knowledge that the Light of Day greets you at the coming dawn.

Though the dance with the Knight may be slow and painful, seemingly never to end, the dancer learns in the process to glide fluidly through the waltz of Life, recognizing that each movement is necessary for the overall dance of the Soul.

Dancing in the Light of Day becomes a joy of glorious proportions when one has completed the Dance through Darkness, with the Knight of Initiation."

-Denise Iwaniw, *A Year of Mystic Angels*

Bringing literary life to his human experiences of death without dying, 16th century Spanish mystic and Doctor of the Roman Church, St. John of the Cross, wrote in his timeless classic, *The Dark Night of the Soul,* "On that glad night, in secret, for no one saw me, nor did I look at anything, with no other light or guide than the one that burned in my heart."

"No other light or guide than the one that burned in my heart."

Those words, potent to my soul, have remained with me for decades.

For me, those words represent a time in each of our lives when we must face the difficult choices that are brought to our path. Most often, we are called to walk the journey of change alone. Whether it is a choice to remain bound to what no longer nourishes us, or a choice to leap from our comfort zone and do what we know within our heart to be right for ourselves and for the good of all, a visit by the ghost of the dark night is simply unavoidable.

Additionally, I happen to believe that the journey through the dark night into the light of a brand new day happens not only for individuals, but also for groups, cities, nations and in fact, the collective consciousness of humanity. Right now, at this precise time on Grandmother Earth, I believe the dark night is taking each and every one of us individually and all of us collectively on a journey deep within the interior castle of ourselves. That very same place that the founder of the Discalced Carmelite Order spoke of … the eternal light and guide that burns *only* in our hearts. It is a grueling journey. Yet, it is always, *always* leads us to a place of greater Light and remarkable wisdom.

One thing we can always be sure of, is that the dark night never travels alone. It will forever haunt us in the company of that most troubling and yet emancipating entity, the Divine Mirror. The Mirror reveals. The Mirror reflects. It pulls the temporary bandages off our wounded places so that true healing can occur. It is our choice to reapply the bandages or to bring our wounding to the Light for healing.

As a species of spiritual beings having human experiences, we are also facing that Mirror, while searching for the indomitable strength of our own eternal, internal Light. We are being asked to stand up and speak up, to let our voices be heard, to let our collective Light shine on the darkness of ignorance, greed, racism, war, poverty, pollution … the list goes on and on. We are being called to be counted, not only for one another, but for all living things. From the protection of our sacred waters at Standing Rock Reservation in North Dakota to human trafficking in Michigan, diamond mining in Africa, global warming, and so much more, we can no longer sit on the fence post and pray that someone on either side will simply take care of what needs to be done for the good of all.

The responsibility of the 7th Generation is to bring about a time of peace, harmony and respect for all living things. It also brings the practicality of assisting in that effort by becoming active and involved in your family, local groups, or the global community. Make a phone call, volunteer your time, and lend some good old fashioned elbow grease or financial resources. During these times, go deep, polish your mirror, work on your personal healing and shine your Light as only you can shine that Light.

Together, we can herald the return of the Light, the likes of which have never been seen or celebrated on Grandmother Earth before.

The time is now. We are the ones we've been waiting for.

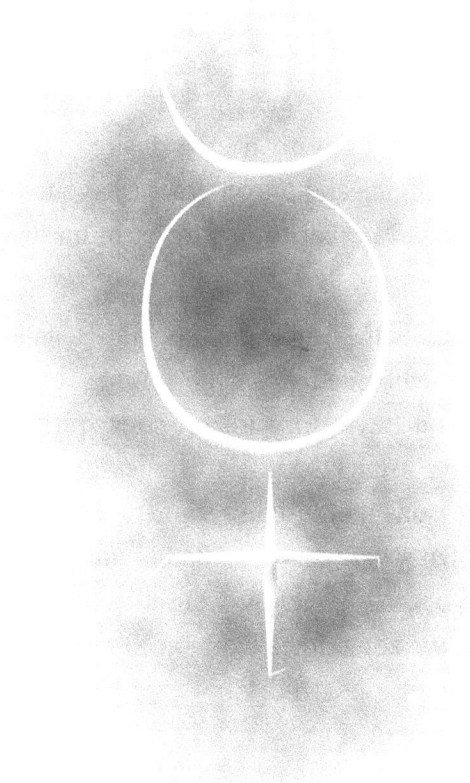

To Everything There is a Season

To everything there is a season,
a time for every purpose under the sun.
A time to be born and a time to die;
a time to plant and a time to pluck up that which is planted;
a time to kill and a time to heal ...
a time to weep and a time to laugh;
a time to mourn and a time to dance ...
a time to embrace and a time to refrain from embracing;
a time to lose and a time to seek;
a time to rend and a time to sew;
a time to keep silent and a time to speak;
a time to love and a time to hate;
a time for war and a time for peace.

Ecclesiastes 3:1-8

Welcome and farewell. Two very potent words that describe not only the changing of seasons around Grandmother Earth, but the change of seasons that each of us experiences in our personal, professional and spiritual lives.

During the advent of summer in North America, I am reminded that as I sow, I am asking the Universe to help me grow. Planting the seeds of my heart's desire in the fertile soil of spring, I watch as new life begins to emerge from the thoughts and prayers that I have lovingly watered with patience and trust. Once again, I am witness to the decay that begins to set in on the old, providing compost for the steady growth of the new.

The mystic journey also brings with it, new friends, new teachers, and new colleagues. Life is truly never the same once you have embarked upon the journey of the soul. You will find a gentle shedding of people in your life as you travel forward on your spiritual path. Every person we meet, every person we interact with and love brings the gift of life lessons. Each of these lessons represents a season in your life. Some of these seasons will last a lifetime and others just a short period of time, perhaps just hours. Outdated belief systems that you have had about yourself and about the world around you will also begin to fall away from you. What you were told to believe as a child is not necessarily the truth of who you are today. Yet, we sometimes hang on to hurtful nicknames, religious beliefs and playground events as though they are absolute truths, never to be changed. In every case, bless the lesson and bless the person who has brought it to you. When the lesson is complete, bless the separate paths that must be taken. As you let go, remember to thank the Universe and the Creator of All for the new lessons and new messengers who are coming your way.

Awakening from Spiritual Slumber

One evening, many years ago, I was awakened in the midst of a very deep sleep by the delightful sounds of laughter and giggling from what I perceived to be dozens of young children. Although I could not see them, I clearly heard their joy as it filled my bedroom from the other side of the veil.

Careful not to alarm my dogs, Merlin, and Gabriel James, I laid quietly in my bed and enjoyed listening to the youthful voices that to me, began to sound like a flock of Angels. With my children fast asleep in their bedrooms, and in accordance with the celestial voices increasing in volume and intensity, Merlin and Gabe popped up from their resting place at the foot of my bed and began to bark in the direction of the heavenly laughter that only the three of us could hear. Surprisingly, their barking and yapping did not deter our visitors from Spirit, nor did it wake Dane and Elyse.

Apparently understanding that there was no need to guard their territory, my furry, four-legged little boys retreated from their defensive posture and with their heads cocking to the right and left in quizzical amusement, joined me in listening to the heavenly passersby.

We were mesmerized.

Following several captivating minutes in this state of otherworldly bliss, our divine visit from the realms of light and sound gently ended and my two little terriers fell fast asleep.

I was delighted to have the company of my little wizard, Merlin and his brother the angel boy, Gabriel James, to bask in such a delight with me. Their natural openness and innate knowing about their place in the wheel of life, makes them perfect companions on the Journey.

Humans on the other hand, can often be full of self-doubt and ignorance about their place in the natural scheme of things. From the well-trained masters of Light, to those who walk in crowds of malfeasance, there are varying degrees of what I call, 'humans who have awakened'.

From the moment that we are born, we begin the process of dying and the return to Home, which is Love. That pure, unconditional Love is sometimes called Light. As with all things that are finding their way Home, they look for signs along the way that tell them Home is somewhere near. The moment we take our first breath in human form, the search for Love, which is Home, begins.

Some humans are born into conditions and or families that have forgotten the *true source* of their being. The remembrance of Home in the Love Light has faded from their collective memory. Humans who have not been helped to remember or have not yet embraced their nature as a being of Light and the resplendent power of Love that comes with this acknowledgement, often try to find Love in all the wrong places.

There are those who believe that real power lies in the wielding of energies devoid of Light. Gossip, hatred, racism, bigotry, ignorance, violence, willful harm, manipulation…the list of offenses to our true nature is long. These offenses belong to the realm of those who are, what I call, sleeping.

Ordinary people, living honest, ordinary lives are a beautiful lot. Not having heard the news that they are extraordinary, spiritual beings, often live a life giving their power over to unseen forces or persons that they feel possess 'special' powers or hold status over them. They do not yet realize that they are special too and are gifted with numerous attributes and talents that the world is waiting for them to share.

For those that are generally aware that they have been given a gift of some sort, yet remain untrained, the journey of the adept is just around the corner. If however, they spend their lifetime without seeking further unfoldment and perfection of their Gifts, they are like a rosebud eternally frozen, forever waiting to blossom.

The one who chooses to fully awaken their Gifts, is the human who will begin the process of self-realization and mastery. They will find and encounter numerous teachers during their lifetime to assist them in their spiritual development, while helping them to keep their eye on Love and their footsteps on the path home to Light.

One of my favorite master teachers is the Coptic Master, Hamid Bey. During his lifetime as a prolific author, lecturer, and spiritual leader, he spoke much about the subject of self-mastery and of becoming a Master. "A master is the one who is awake!" is perhaps my most beloved teaching from this wise Egyptian sage.

I believe that when we awaken from the slumber of an ordinary existence, our life becomes extraordinary and we cannot help but see that only Love and Light is real. To me, an awakened person sees that anything other than Love is an illusion that is brought to us as a form of sometimes painful learning that has the potential to help us find our true essence and safe passage Home.

Sometimes called the initiations of life, our trials and triumphs are gifts that are given to us in order to help us master and balance our emotions, our thoughts, our perception of who we are and to overcome our attachment to the material aspects of life. They are gifts that help set us free!

Humans that come to be known as Masters have done just this. They have overcome the trials of water, air, fire, and earth. By emancipating themselves from the fetters of third dimensional thinking, feeling, understanding, and attachments, they ascended into the realization of their true, solar nature and let their true Light shine. They are awake!

Gabriel James 2017

Tintagel's Magnificent Merlin 2017

Šúŋkawakȟáŋ Wówakȟaŋ

Sacred Horse Medicine

Lectus Star, Sonny River and Heaven's Angel are my 'šúŋkawakȟáŋ wówakȟaŋ', which means Sacred Horse Medicine in the Lakota Sioux language. Also known as Tussy, Beau and Heaven, my four-legged paint horse angels are extraordinary doctors of the body, mind, emotions and spirit.

While I have enjoyed riding horses since I was a young girl, it wasn't until my daughter became an equestrian volunteer at the age of 12, and then a competitor on her high school equestrian team, that I actually had a horse of my own. Tussy came first, followed by Beau. Both accompanied Elyse into the equestrian arena to show in Western and English Hunt Seat competition respectively. Watching the three of them perform in the arena was like witnessing poetry in motion. Harmonized movements, intuitive communication and a growing relationship with one another, that at times, took my breath away.

Alone time at the barn with Tussy and Beau helped Elyse through some very rough, formative years. The rollercoaster ride of emotional highs and lows that came with being a teenager in a home with divorced parents, found Elyse in need of therapy that for her, could only be found in the company of her horses. Even now, as an adult, Elyse and Beau still ride together every week, while Tussy has retired to a much deserved life of leisurely brushings, belly scratching and fresh apple treats. To this day, my daughter still remarks that Beau and Tussy continue to be the best listeners and healers that she has ever known.

It was Heaven's dazzling blue eyes that first captured my attention on a bitterly cold winter day in Michigan. As I slowly approached her at the fence line for the very first time, I could feel Heaven's powerful spirit. The closer I got to her, the stronger it became. Sporting the dark brown medicine-hat markings on her beautiful head, and the matching war-shield markings on her chest, I knew that Heaven was extraordinary. *It* was in the air all around her. As a recent rescue and new addition to the herd at Hidden Creek Stables, Heaven was in need of a person. I, weary in spirit, was in need of a horse. The rest, as they say, is history. Ours is a relationship rich in deep conversation, soulful communication and fuzzy horse lip kisses. Heaven has become my soul's mirror and my most precious teacher. She is my medicine.

As a thunder dreamer, Heaven's magnificent soul accompanies me on spiritual journeys beyond the veil. The sound of her thundering hooves upon the etheric landscape is like a clarion call to the spirits of thunder and lightning and a warning to the darkness, that she is my swift and skilled protector.

Meetings with my guides in the transformative realms of the thunder nation are potent. Whether I travel across the veil for personal healing, mystical insight, or sacred ceremony, Heaven helps me to navigate the landscape with ease and shields me from spiritual malfeasance.

In 2016, my non-profit charity, Gathering Thunder Foundation, hosted Horse Nations Day for the youth of the Nottawaseppi Huron Band of the Potawatomi and their elder chaperones. Forty youth and elders joined myself and members of Gathering Thunder at Hidden Creek Stables and Sanctuary. The urban youth, ages 3 to 15, spent an entire morning with my three painted horses along with a dozen assorted ponies and horses who also call Hidden Creek their home. A rare opportunity for the inner city youth, it was also a rare and priceless opportunity for the Šúŋkawakȟáŋ Wówakȟaŋ Oyáte, the members of the Sacred Horse Nation to be with so many precious Native American youth.

The healing, mutual compassion and boundless joy that took place between the young ones and the horses that day was life changing for everyone who witnessed it. The day was best described by the beautiful young girl who quickly bonded with my Heaven. "Denise, I'm pretty sure my life will never be the same after today. What I felt from the horses was so beautiful and loving. I feel strong now." I replied that I was certain that the horses felt just the same way about spending time with all of them; stronger and more loved than ever before.

Tussy, Elyse, me and Heaven

My Pilgrimage to Chateau de Montsegur

Its name means, 'Safe Mountain' and so it was, that Chateau de Montsegur was created to be a secure dwelling place for the Pure Ones, the Cathars, to live in peace, to keep alive the old ways, all the while perfecting themselves in the Light they knew as God.

For centuries, these keepers of the uncontaminated and ancient spiritual wisdoms did just that. They lived in peaceful harmony with nature, the seen and unseen. Many were commoners with uncommon spiritual gifts. Some were of royal lineage, said to be that of St. Mary Magdalene herself. They were priests, healers, prophets, teachers, and the faithful, who still, after nearly being wiped out during the Inquisition, managed to leave us with the priceless treasures of their wisdom.

On the summer solstice of 2014, I, along with 21 others Mystic Travelers, found myself in France, standing in a most beautiful, fragrant and serene meadow, located at the base of what now remains of Chateau de Montsegur. This sacred field, now covered in yellow, pink and lavender flowers was once the sight of a heinous, mass murder. Yet, only the octaves of love and peace could be felt there in that meadow. Our group had come not only to pray for the over 200 victims who, at the behest of officials from the Church of Rome, were collectively burned alive at the stake one day after celebrating Easter in 1244, but to also give thanks for their legacy and the treasure of their wisdom which is still found hidden in Templar Cathedrals, stained glass windows, the tarot, and in the air of those places once traveled by them, the Cathar Perfects. Those with eyes to see, still see. Those with ears to hear, still hear. Those with an open heart, still understand. The Creator is love and Light and wherever love and Light exist, Creator is there…in all things.

Following our moment of gratitude and prayer in the meadow, those of us who trekked to the top of Montsegur, taking the very same cliff side trail that had been used for centuries by our Cathar ancestors, were awestruck at the raw beauty of the scenery all around us. With the gentle sound of cowbells ringing in the farm pastures well below us, the trees along our path were calmly sharing their memories of this place with us, in a language all their own. All the while, the symbolic paintings and etchings still found on the age old stones along the incredibly steep trail, told us that were ascending in the right direction.

Finally reaching the top of the mountain and the interior of the castle remains, I was deeply moved to be standing under the searing sun and in the very place where well over 200 people were told to recant their Cathar faith or perish by fire. Vacillating between anger and sadness, my feelings and my soul landed in a place of even deeper faith; that place of knowing that it was from the Light that I became and to that very same Light I will one day, like all living things, return.

At one time, the expression of such gifts, *the charismata,* may very well have cost us our earthly lives. Thanks to the legacy of the Cathars and others like them, both past and present, we are made to understand that *we* and our connection to Creator, are the grail treasure that we have been searching for and that this very treasure, lies deep within each and every one of us.

Mountain top view from inside the Chateau de Montsegur Ruins, France 2014

The Uniqueness of Your Soul

It is my belief that each of us is God in expression upon the earth plane.

Our spirit, hurled forth from the center of Creation; the heart and mind of All That Is, born into a human body to fully experience life here on earth with all of its joys and pains, foibles and quirks, imperfections and perfection, is courageous. Because we are related to all things seen and unseen, human life is a passion play that informs all of Creation about the infinite nuances of life as we individual souls dance within the confines of flesh and bone. What we do with the precious gift of our earthly life matters to all.

We are what the stars are made of.

Like the brilliant stars, countless and yet each beloved, that are continuously shining and undulating in the vast expanse of Creations cosmic universes, we too, are assigned to touch earth, to shine, with our own rare and unique formula of stardust and soul wisdom.

The great awakening that is now taking place upon, within and around Grandmother Earth, bids each of us to rise from our slumber. We are being asked to rise and shine in our own distinct radiance and to share our gifts with the world. Some of us are feeling gentle nudges from Spirit that the time is *now* to express our talents, share our stories, lend a hand and volunteer, or to become quiet and listen to and trust the still small voice within. Many are feeling the effects of a cosmic thwack that will not let them rest until they unfetter themselves from whatever or whoever has been holding them back from fully expressing their heart, mind and soul.

The time has come to remove the masks that have hidden us from the sun and to shine like never before. Our spirit guides and guardian angels are waiting with great, joyful anticipation! They support and encourage us from the unseen worlds of the Divine.

In a time where conformity is appealing to many for its security and commonality, celebrating and shining our uniqueness is one of the greatest gifts that we can give to one another. As each of us shines, we invite others to do the same. We give permission to those around us to be who they truly are, each time we lovingly acknowledge and celebrate the exceptional uniqueness in one other.

Planting Seeds

Farmer's markets, with their abundance of freshly harvested vegetables, colorful and ripened fruits, fragrant flowers and homemade jams are a much anticipated autumn treat here in the village that I call home. Strolling through the crowded rows of hopeful vendors, tasting samples of their harvest, chatting with new friends while enjoying the smell of freshly baked goods in the crisp fall air … these are some of my favorite days.

With each passing year, I become more mindful of the springtime labor that precedes these precious autumn mornings. The labor of love that began with seeds, faith and weathered hands; resulting in a bountiful harvest that is brought to my town, piled high in wooden crates in the back of well-worn pickup trucks and farm trailers.

I've also come to realize that I can sense the energy of the very hands and the heart that planted, nurtured and harvested the home grown bounty painstakingly displayed on the market tables. I can feel the vitality of the land that gave birth to the yield.

Instinctively, I am drawn to the tables where my intuition tells me, I will find the results of labors performed with joy.

Cherokee tomatoes are to me, garden treasures. Cherokee tomatoes bursting forth with a ripeness of Light fill my senses and my body with a goodness that is found only in fruit that had its origins in good thoughts, meticulous nurturance and gratitude for its realization.

With each passing year, I become more mindful of the labor that precedes the precious goodness in my life and even of the labor that comes before the sometimes difficult life lessons that I must learn.

Like the blue lotus blossom that pushes through the dark sediment of the Nile River basin, rising ever upward through the rapidly flowing waters to taste the life giving the rays of the sun, each of us is a flower in Creator's garden. As Creator in expression, every one of us is constantly creating.

Our thoughts and words, like garden seeds planted in springtime, have the potential to bear fragrant fruit or create insidious poisons. Like our human children, our thoughts and words, born of our mind, our pen and our tongue, become our responsibility once we have given birth to them.

Sometimes referred to as the children of our mind, the energies that we release into the creative matrix of the universe take on a life of their own. When fed and nurtured, they continue to grow and soon become independent of us. Many, like the Sufi master, Hafiz, the beloved Mother Theresa or the American philosopher, Joseph Campbell, have left behind a legacy of thoughtful progenies that continue to help shape a more loving world. Others, leave in their wake a brood of children that represent the spirit of fear, ignorance, waste and hopelessness.

When your season of harvest approaches and the final strokes of the universal pen compose the closing chapters in the book of your life, will others look at your children and remark that you raised them well? Will you have left in your wake a legacy that nourishes and enriches generations yet to come? Will your volumes be entitled, *The Book of the Living* or *The Book of the Dead*?

Light Showers

"Blessed are they who endeavor to find the Light,

… though they walk through the shadow of the

illusion known as darkness.

They understand their *True* nature.

Blessings be to those who show the Way,

and hold the hearts of those lost

in darks' illusion.

They are the *Light show-ers*.

Blessings rain upon those who *hold* the Light,

despite the illusion of chaos.

They understand that *all* things emanate

from the *Great Lightness*."

-Denise Iwaniw-Francisco

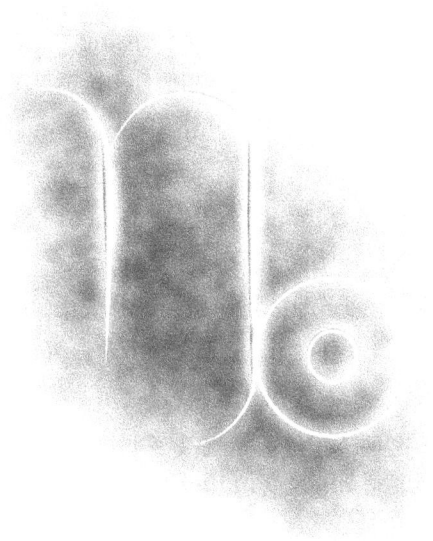

Creating Sacred Spaces for Prayer and Ceremony

Before you begin any type of sacred work, be sure to dress comfortably and carefully choose an appropriate place to relax into your prayers or to hold ceremony. Invite your celestial companions to join you as you seek to hold divine conversation and receive spiritual guidance. Call upon your Guardian Angels, Spirit Guides, and even your Totem Spirit Animals to be with you. Light a candle and give thanks for the company of these teachers and for the divine guidance you are about to receive.

Just as we appreciate a thank-you, so too do our heavenly companions. You may also use a bit of incense or essential oils to balance the energy of your sacred space. I recommend sage, cedar, sweet grass, rose, copal, sandalwood or frankincense and myrrh. The essence of these scents carries a very high vibration. As their vibration is released into the air, it dissipates any lower vibrations that may be in the area and at the same time raises the vibration to a level conducive to spiritual work.

Some prefer to use drums, rattles, tuning forks or Tibetan or crystal singing bowls to raise the vibrational frequency in a room. Tingsha's are also useful in dispersing lower vibrations and bringing in higher vibrations. Yet others use the ancient method of toning. Several heartfelt "OM's" will immediately set the energy of a room and of your own energy field and prepare you for divine guidance. To mystical Egyptians, sounding the "OM" is a powerful incantation that calls out to the cosmic Mother. Following this, you must take a moment to 'ground' or 'balance' yourself. What is grounding and balancing? Grounding is firmly connecting yourself to the physical realm, such as Mother Earth. You can do this by visualizing tree roots growing out of the bottoms of your feel and going deep down into Mother Earth. Remember when you are finished to bring the tree roots up out of Mother Earth. If you are outdoors you can ground yourself by hugging a tree or by putting your hands in soil. Balancing is about equalizing the energy in and around your body. Having a balanced body, mind, spirit and emotions is essential for being able to hear, see, taste and smell communication from Spirit. It is also required for a stable sense of knowing and understanding Divine communications as they are given.

If group ceremony is being held, it is important to make sure that *all* participants are well grounded and their energy balanced.

At the start of many sacred ceremonies, each participant is 'smudged' or undergoes an energy body cleansing with the use of cedar, sage, sweet grass, copal, or frankincense and myrrh prior to the onset of ceremony. Using a single feather or feather fan to waft the smoke of the botanic or incense smoke around each person, front and back, bottom to top, energetic impurities are washed away and absorbed into ethers.

In some traditions, this form of clearing also takes place during and following ceremony to keep the spaces in and around the ceremony clear and clean. In some ceremonial follow-up, washing hands, elbows and arms with cedar leaf infused water is also employed as a means of undergoing a clearing, particularly in the case of healing ceremonies that require interaction with spirits of a lesser vibration.

According to the Medical Dictionary:

Definition of Smudging (smu-jing). *n*

In Native American medicine, the ritual of purifying the location, patient, healer, helpers and ritual objects by using the smoke obtained by burning sacred plants, such as sage, sweet grass, and cedar. It alters the state of consciousness and enhances sensitivity. This altered sensitivity to imbalances in the spiritual and energetic realm is necessary for the healer to assess and treat an illness. Cleansing often initiates healing sessions.

Growing up in a Catholic family, I have often been witness to another form of smudging that takes place during a Catholic mass. Whether it is during a high ceremony such as a funeral mass, a Holy Day of Obligation, like Ash Wednesday, or a holy day (holiday) such as Easter, a Catholic priest employs his incense burner, known as a censer, to waft the sacred smoke of frankincense and myrrh throughout the church and upon his parishioners. This ancient practice keeps the church sanctuary clear of any and all forms of negativity, allowing the Light of the Divine to prevail and bring harmony to all.

The prayers and incantations contained within these pages are meant to be spoken, chanted or sung from the beauty of your heart.

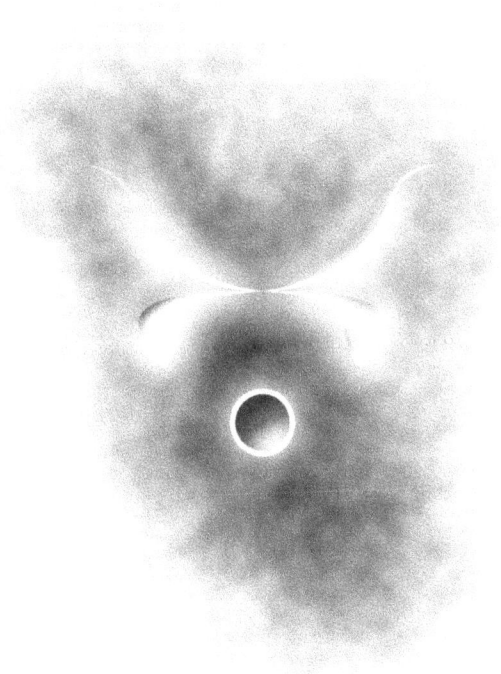

Prayers

The Tor of St. Michael, Glastonbury, England. Solstice, 2016

Prayer to Our Lady of the Light

Prayer to Our Lady of the Light

Blessed Mother,

Beloved creatrix of All Things

good and loving,

Birther of Light,

thank you for helping me

to *see* your Light

and Love

in *all* things,

including *me*.

Help me to shine my Light

as only *I* can shine;

a living,

loving,

expression

of *You*.

Amen.

Our Lady of St. Nons, Wales, 2016

Blue Thunder Prayer

Blue Thunder Prayer

Summoning the Seven Sacred Winds

"Sacred winds of the West, lead me to the voices and to the wisdom

of my ancestors.

Help me to hear them speaking to my Spirit."

"Sacred winds of the North, lead me safely through the winters of Life.

Help me to remain strong."

"Sacred winds of the East, lead me to the source of my inner sun.

Help me to listen and follow the teachings of my Heart."

"Sacred winds of the South, lead me to my Purpose.

Help me to remain on my Soul's True Path."

"Sacred winds of the Star Nations, lead me to the heart and mind of Creator.

Help me to understand this kind of Love."

"Sacred winds of the Good Spirits, lead me to understand the Seen and Unseen.

Help me to live in balance between both worlds."

"Sacred winds of Grandmother Earth, lead me to walk my earth journey in a Good Way.

I am related to all living things."

Devil's Tower, Wyoming USA

Sacred Waters

Sacred Waters

White Buffalo Calf Woman

Mother of the Stars,

Goddess of Light,

Holy Woman of the Red Road Way;

You are The One whose face appears

in the rainbows

and rain,

thunder clouds

and lightning,

rivers and streams,

oceans and seas,

in the depths my psyche and soul,

and in wellspring of my tears.

I feel you nourishing my body.

I sense you dancing in my mind.

I *know* you in my soul.

I love you.

I honor you.

I am grateful for your holy Presence in the Sacred Waters

that nourish *all* of Life.

Thank you for flowing clearly and effortlessly

through me,

so that the essence of all that I AM

is an earthly expression of the eternal love of *You*.

Bare Bones

"Sometimes life renders us down to our bare bones

so that we can *begin* once again,

to see the path of our Soul with a clean, clear view…

one that is *unfettered* by the past,

unconcerned with the future,

and fully *awake* to the gift of the present moment."

-Denise Iwaniw-Francisco

St. John's Episcopal Church, Oglala, South Dakota USA
Pine Ridge Indian Reservation 2013

Healing the Past

Healing the Past

Divine Mother

Cosmic Birther and lover of all things;

help me to love my very Soul,

my Soul's twisty, turning path,

and the many initiations of my Soul.

Thank you for helping me to understand

that every fire I have passed through,

every perceived loss that I have suffered

was a gift to bring me closer to you;

only to bring me closer to Me.

In the scorched places, please soothe me.

In the empty places, please fill me.

In the lonely places, please come near me.

In the angry places, please heal me.

In the unforgiving places, please help me to understand.

Thank you for helping me to see that healing my past,

means healing the *now* in me.

Amen.

Releasing that Which No Longer Serves the Path of My Soul

Releasing that Which No Longer Serves the Path of My Soul

The ties that bind me,

to the past, to the hurts,

to the chains of relationships lost,

now release me.

The love ties,

the lie ties,

the ties that once served me well,

are now untied.

The useless bonds,

the harmful bonds,

the bonds of impending decay and death,

are now unbound.

I am free.

My outstretched arms

ready to receive,

hungry for the new,

joyfully wrap themselves around my Soul's journey.

I am ready to let go.

I am ready and grateful to receive.

I am alive once more!

Amen.

Warrior's Prayer

A Warrior's Prayer

Angelic Legions of Light

of Protection,

and of Love,

thank you for leading,

over-lighting,

and safe guarding

my loved one.

Thank you for watching over them

while they are away,

and for guiding them safely home

to family, friends,

and a place of deep, abiding rest

when their tour of duty is done.

Amen.

Prayer for Veterans

Prayer for Veterans

Creator,

Loving Source of Life,

Birther of Warriors,

and their Sacred Heart

of Compassion,

forged

by the fires of war,

and the *duality* of Love,

help them to heal.

Bathe them in Your Holy Light of unconditional Love.

Free them from the ghosts of death and destruction,

and restore them to Your joy.

Ease the endless chatter of their mind,

and bring serenity to the haunted corridors of their spirit.

Bring them to, and hold them in Your loving peace;

a peace that surpasses all earthly understanding.

So it is.

Amen.

Prayer for the Land

Prayer for the Land

Creator of *all*,

earth and sky,

grasses and trees,

flora and fauna,

rivers and streams,

oceans and seas,

mountains and deserts,

above and below,

I am grateful.

Thank you for the gift of life

that is contained in all that my eyes can see,

that my ears can hear,

my hands can touch,

and my heart can feel.

Thank you for showering your blessings of love, nourishment and abundance

upon this land,

and all who live upon, within and above it;

both seen and unseen.

So it is,

that we are *all* blessed by You

as you bless this land.

Amen.

Prayer for World Peace

Prayer for World Peace

Creator of the Universes,

Cosmos,

Galaxies,

and Grandmother Earth,

rain Your never-ending peace upon this blue green planet,

and within the hearts and minds

of humanity.

Bring us to the understanding

that we are all related.

Help us to know that what we do to one,

we do to all,

including ourselves.

In the ignorant places, bestow Your wisdom.
In the hateful places, deliver Your love.
In the unforgiving places, bring Your understanding.
In the blinded places, make us to see through Your eyes,

and know that *all* that is seen and *unseen*

is a holy expression of You;

the One love

the *breath*

that brings all things to life.

Your peace now reigns, forever and ever.

Amen.

Prayer for a Gentle Transition

Winds of Change,

of transformation,

transfiguration,

and new life,

thank you

for

this gentle transition

from what was,

to what is,

and what shall be.

Thank you for your net of love

that will carry me

joyfully, peacefully, and gently

to what is next,

on this

exquisitely joyful,

excruciatingly painful,

breathtakingly beautiful,

journey of my Soul.

All is well and as it should be.

Amen.

Prayer for a Restless Spirit

Prayer for a Restless Spirit

Restless Spirit

wandering Soul,

may you find infinite peace

in the arms of

Love;

the everlasting tenderness

of all that is,

has ever been,

and forever shall be.

Immortal Angels of

Perpetual Light,

bring all restless and earthbound spirits

to the center of Creation,

the Heart and Mind of God,

where all goodness

and love dwells,

and has its undying way.

Bring them to peace.

So be it.

Amen.

Prayer for Entering the Dreamworld

Prayer for Entering the Dreamworld

Dreamtime guardians,

keepers of the

unseen lands of myth,

memories,

mysteries,

and muse,

thank you for welcoming me

into the depths of my psyche,

and of my very soul.

Stalwart regents who oversee the

kingdoms of angels and demons alike,

guard and guide my spirit

through the troublesome terrains of shadow,

into the realms of pure Love,

and heavenly Light.

Escort me to the schools of eternal wisdom

that lie deep within

the heart and mind of God.

Let my soul take rest there,

in the bosom of the Mother.

Help me to remember

my beauty, my eternity,

and the Love from which I was born.

I am grateful.

Blessings be.

Releasing Worry

Releasing Worry

Knowing that I AM a Divine Expression of God

A Beloved of the One

I release all worry

to the unified field of the Creator's love;

where my uncertainty in life's perfection

will be transmuted into trusting

that my life is divinely guided,

that I am supported by the Universe,

that I walk in the company of God's angels of light,

that my life has purpose,

and that every moment of my life is perfectly woven

with the splendid threads of Creator's love.

I know that all is well

and all manner of things are perfectly well.

So it is.

Ancient Monolith Stones at Carnac, France 2014

Going with the Flow

"Sometimes…

the best *plan*

is to simply go

with the flow."

-Denise Iwaniw-Francisco

Nag Hammadi Mountain Range, Nag Hammadi, Egypt, 2009

Gratitude

Gratitude

Divine Light
home to my soul
source of my love
animator of my spirit
I am grateful.

Cosmic Mind
Seer
Seeker
Revealer
Lover
Strength
Indwelling of God
I am grateful.

Let me know,
let me see,
let me find,
let me reveal,
let me love,
let me feel,
You
and Me.

Blessings be.

Prayer for Mealtime

Prayer for Mealtime

Holy Mother,

Divine Father,

Creator of my physical body,

and the food that I am prepared to eat,

thank You for blessing this meal

with your endless Love,

and abundant Light.

Thank you for showering blessings upon

all who have prepared this meal,

and the beings that have given of themselves

to make it so.

I am grateful

for this nourishment,

and I am grateful for You.

So it is.

Amen.

Healing Addictions

Healing Addictions

Spirits of addiction,

I release you.

Spirits of compulsion,

you no longer serve me.

Love now dwells

in the empty places that your spirits once filled.

Light now dwells

in the darkened spaces of fear that were once occupied by you.

Joy now dwells

in the bitter places that your angered spirits once held.

Hope now dwells

in the corridors of despair where you once stood.

Healing and wholeness now prevail

where you once lived.

Spirits of addiction

I now send you to the Light

the source of all Love.

I am whole.

So it is.

Amen.

Prayer for Sobriety

Prayer for Sobriety

Spirits of Addiction

Specters of Bondage and Pain

leave me.

Angels of Sobriety

Messengers of Wholeness and Light

heal me.

Holy Mother

Sacred Heart of Light and Love

fill me.

Creator of All Things

Good and Holy

Embrace me.

Sacred Self

The Essence of Who I AM

over-light me.

I am released, I am filled, I am embraced, I am healed,

I am joyful, I am sober and I am loved,

by the One Light.

I AM the Light.

So it is.

Amen.

Healing Ancestral Trauma

Healing Ancestral Trauma

Angels of restorative Light,

thank you for healing the cosmic thread that weaves

itself through my family tree,

bringing us peace, hope, abundance and joy.

Grandmothers and grandfathers

thank you for receiving this prayerful healing

of the events that have rendered your People unwell.

Ancestors of my blood,

memories of my marrow,

together, we now release all traumas

still resonating through Time.

Throughout time,

and in the flow of our ancestral blood, body, spirit and mind,

we are now whole, healthy, safe and loved.

Amen.

Our Lady of St. Labre Indian School,
Ashland, Montana USA 2012

Healing Cellular Memories

Holy Mother, Divine Father

Cosmic Birther of All things,

thank you for helping me to remember

that you and I are One.

You are the Source of my being,

the Joy of my heart,

and the Origin of my soul.

In this knowledge,

the cellular memories of all that has been

unloving, unjust, unhealthy, and unsound

are now made clear within me.

I have lovingly cultivated each diamond

that my life experiences have gifted me.

You and I are One.

You and I are Source.

Together, We are Joy,

and I am whole.

Peace be.

The sacred Sweetgrass Hills,
Montana, USA 2016

Deep Thirst

"The Seeker often thirsts so *deeply* for union with the *One*

that they must set out on an epic journey that only *they* can take.

Alone, with *faith* as their solitary companion,

the ascent toward wholeness finds them leaving all

of their *earthly* belongings behind,

rendering their soul *naked* to the elements of *Truth*.

With nothing left to shield them

from the onslaught of the *winds*, the *rains*, the *trembling* and the *heat*

of the desert sands,

they come to meet the One who did not hold their hand *without*,

but the One who is the Eternal Light *within*.

They see the *Truth* of the Union with the *One*."

-Denise Iwaniw-Francisco

Prayer for the Animals

Prayer for the Animals

Mother, Father God,

Creator of All things good and loving,

thank you for your Gift of the four legged,

the winged ones,

the swimmers,

and the creepy crawlers.

Thank You for keeping all of your beloved creatures safe from harm.

When they are hungry, thank You for providing them with nourishing food.

When they are thirsty, thank You for providing them with clean water.

When they are lonely, thank You for providing them with loving companionship.

When they are homeless, thank You for providing them with safe harbor.

When they are wandering, thank You for giving them guidance.

When they are diseased, thank You for bringing them to wellness.

When they are ready to come home to You,

thank You for sending your Angels of Light to receive them.

In the sacred web of Life,

we are all related to You,

and we are loved.

Amen.

Horse Nation Prayer

Horse Nation Prayer

Horse Nation,

thundering guides,

gentle healers,

mirrors of truths,

thank you for bringing me

to the center of my Self.

Thank you for showing me

how to be strong, yet, gentle.

Thank you

for helping me

to be unfettered and free.

I am grateful for your friendship,

compassion, and unconditional love.

Holy Mother,

Divine Father,

Creator of All Things,

thank you for the gift of the horse nation.

Protect them from all harm,

neglect,

ignorance,

and abuse.

Thank you for nourishing them,

as they, *selflessly*

nourish me.

Amen.

Morning Prayer

Morning Prayer

Angels of the morning sun

divine ministers of dawn,

whose brilliant rays arrive upon the life-giving breath of Creation

I welcome the gift of this new day.

Thank you for bringing with you new opportunities

to play

to forgive

to love

to learn

to grow

to live

to be your eyes

your heart

your ears

and your hands on Earth.

Creator of All Things,

I am grateful for this day.

I am grateful for my life.

I am grateful for you.

Amen.

Mid-Day Prayer

Mid-Day Prayer

Angels of the midday sun

glorious orb of golden light

caressing the blueness of midday sky

thank you for the gift of your radiant light.

Thank you for the gift of your nourishing rays.

Thank you for banishing the shadows

revealing the truth of my own inner light.

Glorious Father Sun

thank you for helping to reveal the light within me

and for helping me to see the beauty of your Light,

which dwells in all things,

including me.

Amen.

Evening Prayer

Evening Prayer

Angels of the evening Light

revealers of the midnight sun,

of the evening stars,

thank you for reflecting to me the abundant blessings in my life

the blessing *of* my life

and the deep love of the Mother and the Father,

for having breathed and exhaled my soul into Life.

Light rays of the evening sun,

revealers of all that has been,

sentinels of what is to come,

I am grateful for this day.

For the knowledge that I have gained,

the beauty that was revealed,

and the love that I have experienced through all that Creator has made

I am thankful.

I am grateful for my life

I am grateful for the evening sky

I am grateful for you.

Amen.

Restorative Sleep

Restorative Sleep

Nocturnal guardians

Angels of spiritual restoration

and of deep, healing sleep,

thank you for helping me to calm my unsettled mind,

and bring harmony to my troubled Spirit.

Thank you for relieving me of physical discomfort

and the concerns of my heart.

Angels of the Dream world,

deliver me to the source of the Creator's calm.

Lift me into the loving arms of the Divine Mother of All.

Rock me in the cradle of Creations' vast, Cosmic Sea,

and bring me to Its center of Silent Peace

Guide me, guard me and sing me into a deep, restorative sleep.

Amen.

Monet's Garden, Giverny, France 2014

Prayer for Strength and Courage

Prayer for Strength and Courage

Mighty Lioness

Lady of Courage

Strength of my Heart

Fill me with your unconquerable Light.

Breathe your loving strength into every ounce of my being.

Holy Father

Creator of All Things

Courage of My Soul

Fill me with your eternal Light.

Breathe your loving courage into every ounce of my being.

Take from me all that binds my soul to weakness, discouragement, doubt and fear.

Fill me with Your Love.

Amen.

The Sphinx, Giza, Egypt 2009

Don't Just Stare

"Don't stare

at the closed door

too long.

You'll miss

the window

opening before you."

-Denise Iwaniw-Francisco

Tintern Abbey Ruins, Wales, 2016

A Heart that is Open

A Heart that is Open

Heart of the Universe

Divine Wisdom

Mother;

help me to open my heart

to the loving warmth and wisdom

of You.

Beloved Sophia,

Protectress of Love,

assure my heart that the love of You

shall always prevail;

in the dark places,

fearful places,

doubtful places,

wounded places,

and the corridors of my loves' despair.

Strengthen my heart with your courage, resilience, trust and delight.

Thank you for helping me to live a life that joyfully engages

and deeply nourishes my heart

and yours.

Amen.

An Open Mind

An Open Mind

Divine Mind,

Universal Consciousness,

Creatrix of Heaven and Earth,

thank you for helping me to see,

to hear,

to feel,

this human life

unperturbed by the turbulence of my brain,

the sorrow of my experiences,

or the prejudices of my little mind.

Bring healing to the chaotic places,

the solemn places,

the arrogant places,

the hurtful places

all of the places not fully connected

to You.

So it is. Blessings be.

Tatanka on Sacred Bear Butte, South Dakota, USA, 2011

The Seer

"When the Seer begins to *see*

with a balanced heart

and mind…

all that is to be seen,

begins to *see*

the Seer."

-Denise Iwaniw-Francisco

Inípi, Purification Lodge, 2017

An Open Third Eye

An Open Third Eye

All Seeing

Love of the Universe,

thank you for helping me to see

my life,

my experiences,

my spirit,

my soul,

your Angels,

the ancients,

and their timeless wisdom,

through Your eyes;

the eyes of unconditional love,

that see within, without and beyond the veil,

that allow me to see all of the infinite expressions

and experiences

of You which are Me.

Through you,

I see

all things

clearly.

So it is.

Amen.

Receiving

Bountiful Universe,

Bestower of all things Light and Loving;

thank you.

Arms that were once clenched in unworthiness

are now open.

A heart once fearful to welcome love

is now available to receive.

A mind once damaged by betrayal and abuse

now trusts.

A past riddled with shame

now sees the beauty of the lessons learned.

As I give

all unworthiness, fear, betrayal, abuse, shame and doubt to You,

I receive

the Love of the Universe;

of You

ten thousand fold.

My life is abundant.

I am open to receive.

So it is.

Amen.

The End

"And in the end,

each of us faces

a glorious new beginning."

-Denise Iwaniw-Francisco

The Chalice Well, Glastonbury, England. Solstice 2016

Light in the Mourning

Light in the Mourning

Holy Light

Holy Mother

Creator of Love

Creator of beginnings

lifetimes and endings;

thank you for holding my heart

in the Light of your Love,

as I walk through the shadow

of death,

and mourning,

remembering,

reconciling,

understanding,

ascending,

rebirthing,

within the Light of You,

into the Light of a new me.

Thank you for gently embracing my soul,

as I pass from death to life.

Amen.

Banishing Negativity

Banishing Negativity

Our Lady of the Angels,

Splendid Light,

thank you for banishing all forms of negativity

from my heart, spirit, mind, body and soul.

Send your holy angels to perfect all spaces around me,

seen and unseen.

Fill me with your luminous love,

and your brilliant courage.

Cause me to shine like the heavenly stars

that embrace your skyward Being.

Make me a vehicle of your resplendent Light

and an eternal repository of your love,

where no evil would ever chance to dwell.

So it is.

Amen.

Tobernalt Holy Well, Sligo, Ireland 2016

Eternal Soul

"Our soul,

like our *love* for one another,

is an *endless...timeless...eternal...*Gift,

from the *One,*

who loves us

most of all."

-Denise Iwaniw-Francisco

Upper Panther Meadows, Mount Shasta, California, USA

Death without Dying

Death without Dying

Angels of Death

Life,

and the spaces in between,

I acknowledge the eternity of

my Self.

Forever changing

in thought form,

perpetually growing from the decay of the old,

I live and live again.

I am eternal,

shifting only in form

throughout the Ages.

I cannot die.

For I am Life itself.

I AM alive.

And so it is.

Peace be.

I AM

I stopped to ask my Self, "What AM I?"

A silent voice from deep within ME answered …

"I AM a Child of the Light

I AM the Light

I AM a Child of the One Love

I AM that Love

I AM a Child of the Stars

I AM the Stars

I AM here to Shine."

"I AM here on Earth to Shine my Light, my Love,

my Stardust.

I am here to Shine!"

-Denise Iwaniw-Francisco

Goddess Seshat, Temple of Horus, Edfu, Egypt, 2006

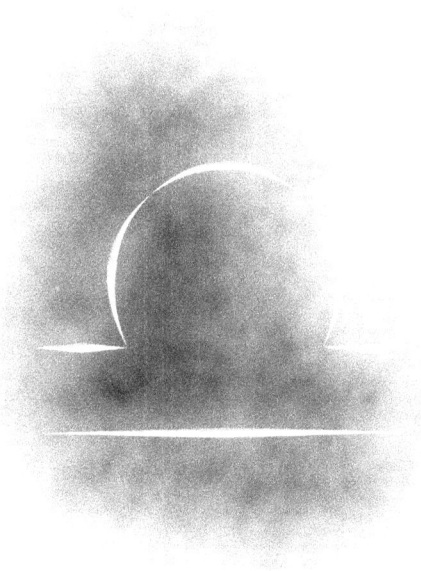

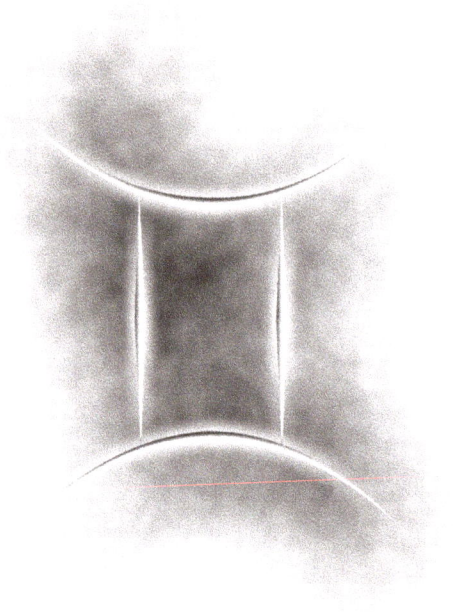

Incantations

Stonehenge, England 2016

Incantation to the Mother

Incantation to the Mother – Litany of Her Holy Names

Queen of the Heavens
Our Lady of the Stars
Cosmic Birther
Earthly Mother
Mediatrix of Heaven and Earth
Our Lady of the Oceans
Mother of the Seas
Divinity of Water
Sacred Heart of Love
Lady of Wisdom
Mother of Compassion
Giver of Life
Black Madonna
Spirit of the Wind, Earth, Water and Fire
Protectress of Children
Our Lady of Time
She Who Sees All Things
Divine Mother of All
Light of Splendor
Mother of Ascension
Sophia Divine
Our Lady of the Angels
Lioness of Courage
Our Lady of the Moon
Mother of the Sun
Queen of All Nations
Our Lady of the Spheres
Splendid Lady of Nature
Loving Mother of All That Lives
Spirit of Joy,
perfume this sacred space.

Divine Weaver
Heavenly Love
Blessed Mother
fill me
with Your love.

So it is.
Blessings be.

Incantation to the Goddess

Incantation to the Goddess – She Who Has Many Faces and Names

Aphrodite
Artemis
Astarte
Butterfly Maiden
Bastet
Baba Yaga
Brigit
Danu
Demeter
Diana
Freya
Fortuna
Gaia
Hecate
Inanna
Isis
Ix Chel
Kali
Kuan Yin
Lilith
Mary
Morning Star Woman
Nut
Ostara
Parvati
Pele
Sekmet
Shakti
Shekinah
Sophia
Tara
Venus
White Buffalo Calf Woman
Mother of All,
please come and bless this sacred space,
with your wisdom and insight,
with your love, endless compassion and peace.
So it is. Blessings be.

The Alchemy of Incantations and the Sacred Directions

Rituals and sacred ceremonies are typically created to consist of three main parts; the opening, the ceremony itself and the closing. Whether in a group or utilizing incantations alone, being mindful and joyful during every aspect of ceremony is important to the overall experience.

By focusing your body position and attention on each of the sacred directions as they are called, an energetic connection is made and a beautiful bridge is built between the physical and non-physical realms.

The most important thing to remember is to be of light heart. This is after all, a special time for you to connect with Creator and Creation in a way that is nourishing to your soul. Let your spirit lead the way!

Earlier in the book, I wrote about the creation of a sacred space for ceremony to take place. Now, let's take a look at the three components of the ceremony itself.

The opening:

When standing in sacred space, and when possible, please face and connect with each of the four directions in a clockwise manner, as well as the direction of the sky (when appropriate) as you call them in. In recognizing the direction of in-between, you may wish to extend your hand out in front of you at the level of your abdomen, and when addressing Grandmother Earth, you may wish to touch the ground.

Whether standing or sitting during the opening of ceremony, take the time necessary to *feel* each of the energies of the Sacred Directions as they are called upon. Remember to breathe.

The Ceremony:

A sacred ceremony can be as simple or complex as you desire. The recitation of a single prayer or incantation can suffice to create a spectacular union with the Divine. Adding sacred song, movement, music, chant, or teachings to a ceremony is certainly a wonderful way to further deepen the ceremonial experience.

The Closing:

Closing a ceremony is a creative process as well. Often times, when the sacred directions have been invoked in a clockwise fashion during the opening, some people prefer to then close ceremony by giving gratitude to the elements of those same sacred directions, but in reverse order.

The singing of a song, recitation of a fitting prayer, and words of gratitude are also a fine way to wrap up a time of sacred space.

Incantation to the Light of the Seven Sacred Directions

Incantation to the Light of the Seven Sacred Directions

Ancestral Light of the West;

I call to you.

Hidden Light of the North;

I call to you.

New Light of the East;

I call to you.

Healing Light of the South;

I call to you.

Guiding Light of the Starry Skies;

I call to you.

Invisible Light of the In-between;

I call to you.

Nurturing Light of Grandmother Earth;

I call to you.

Hear my call, come to me. Be present in this sacred space,

to teach

to reveal

to renew

to heal

to guide

to balance

to nurture

Light within and without, come to help me *see*.

Seven Sacred Winds

Incantation to the Seven Sacred Winds

I call to the winds of the West,

home of the ancestors, the thunderers, buffalo and horse. Welcome.

Thank you for helping me to connect with the wisdom of the Old Ones.

I call to the winds of the North,

home of the wolf, elk, salmon and whale. Welcome.

Thank you for helping me to connect with the sacred songs of Creator.

I call to the winds of the East,

home of the eagle, rabbit, bobcat and otter. Welcome.

Thank you for teaching me to see things through the eyes of the Creator.

I call to the winds of the South,

home of the hawk, turtle, rattlesnake and seal. Welcome.

Thank you for helping me to see clearly and to be fearless on my Earth walk.

I call to the winds of In-between,

Home of the holy spirits. Welcome.

Thank you for teaching me your ways of kindness and loving compassion.

I call to the winds of below,

Home of the stones, rocks, minerals and mountains. Welcome.

Thank you for nurturing me with the strength and your ancient stories.

I call to the winds of above,

Home of the star nations, cloud nations, suns and moons. Welcome.

You and I are one.

So it is.

The Four Winds

The Four Winds

Sacred Spirits of the West,

welcome to my Sacred Space.

I am grateful for your wisdom.

Holy Spirits of the North,

welcome to my sacred space.

I am grateful for your peace.

Blessed Spirits of the East,

welcome to my sacred space.

I am grateful for your sustenance.

Divine Spirits of the South,

welcome to my sacred space.

I am grateful for your healing.

Thank you for blessing this space and all who have gathered here.

Lenticular Clouds over Mount Shasta, California, USA

Family

"Each step along the way

made her *realize* ...

that family extends beyond the boundaries

of humanity,

deep into the fertile soil

of Grandmother,

ever upward into the galaxies

of Grandfather,

and to every living thing

that is seen by the eye

and known by the heart."

-Denise Iwaniw-Francisco

Mortuary Temple of Queen Hatshepsut, Valley of the Queens, Egypt, 2009

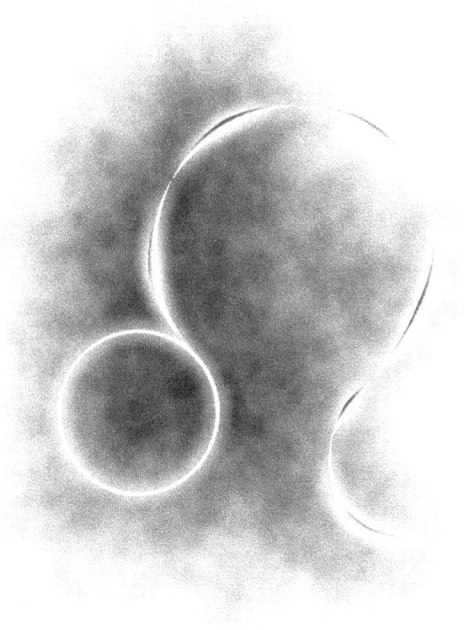

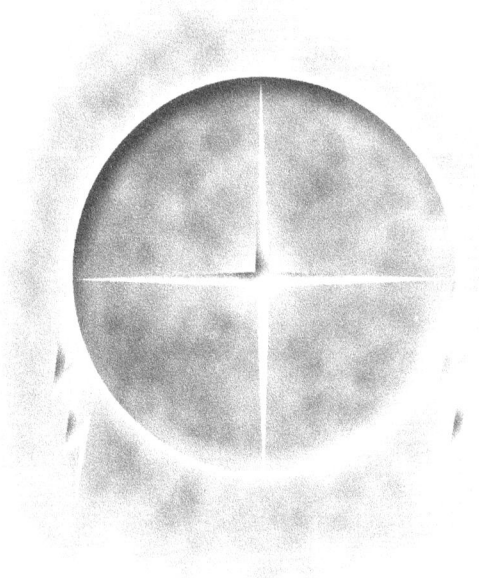

Mother Nature

In Her infinite wisdom, Mother Nature provides us with spiritual insight along the Mystic Journey. The energy of Mother Moon, Father Sun, Brother Wind and Sister Stars affects the rhythm of our own human body. The stages of our life are referred to as seasons.

Glendalough, Ireland, 2016

As with all living things, if you ask Mother Nature for a sign, She will undoubtedly oblige your request. To hear Her answer, you must pay very close attention. As an exercise in this form of communication, take time on a starry night to ask Mother Nature for a sign that you are connected to and supported by Universal Grace. Then pay close attention to the formation of the clouds, the wind, the planets and the stars. You'll be amazed by Her response. While you may not hear Her speak to you in a conventional manner, She will most definitely speak to you in a manner that your Spirit understands.

To many indigenous People, Grandfather Stone is very much alive and full of wisdom. Have you ever been out in nature and come upon a stone that appeared to have a face on it? I have. Looking into the face of Grandfather Stone always makes me smile. When I place my hand upon his surface and listen with my ears, my eyes and my heart, He always tells me a story that my soul needs to hear.

Ibis along the Nile River, Egypt, 2009

Incantation to the Spirits of Nature

Incantation to the Spirits of Nature

Good spirits of the rock, stone and mineral kingdoms,
I call to you. Bring your ancient stories to this sacred space.

Goods spirits of plant, tree, flora and fauna kingdoms,
I call to you. Bring your nurturing breath to this sacred space.

Good spirits of the river, stream, sea and ocean kingdoms,
I call to you. Bring your ancient songs to this sacred space.

Good spirits of the sky, clouds, thunder and lightning worlds,
I call to you. Bring your clear sight to this sacred space.

Good spirits of the sun, stars, moons and galaxies,
I call to you. Thank you for bringing the love of all Creation to this sacred space.

So it is.

Na Pali Coast, Kaua'i, Hawai'i, 2013

Incantation to the Sun

Incantation to the Sun

Celestial Orb
of Light Supreme
Bringer of Light,
of warmth,
of Life,
welcome to this sacred space.

Moon's lover,
Father Sun,
Eastern Sphere,
come.
Penetrate the Darkness.

Bring your Light,
Your Love,
Your Life,
Your Hope,
to me.

So it is.

Inside Rosslyn Chapel, Midlothian
Scotland, 2012

Incantation to the Moon

Incantation to the Moon

Mother,
Goddess,
Mirror of Truths,
Sophia of my Self,
welcome to this sacred space.

Orb of Oracles,
Midnight Sun,
Keeper and Revealer of Secrets,
come.

Help me to *see*,
to *feel*,
to *hear*,
to *know*,
Creators loving thoughts of Me.
So it is.

Temple of Horus at Edfu, Egypt 2009

Incantation to the Stars

Incantation to the Stars

The Litany of Mystical Light

Venus, Orion

Polaris and Pleiades,

Alpha Centauri, Sirius

Aquarius and Corvus,

Betelgeuse, Cetus

Pegasus and Leo,

Cassiopeia, Rigel

Ursa Major the Bear,

Lepus, Lupus

Serpens and Antares,

Delphinus, Virgo

Aquarius and Cancer,

Cygnus, Canis Major

Scorpius and Lynx,

Aquila the Eagle and bringer of Light;

the Sun.

Shine your wisdom, sing your songs, speak to my Spirit, and nurture my Soul.

Tell me of my origins, teach me about me.

In the Great Weave of Galaxies and Universes

and in the Web of all Life

we are One.

And so it is. Blessings be.

Caring for Sacred Objects

When was the last time you cleaned your crystals, washed your sacred stones, soaked your talismans in the sunlight, or filled your feathers with the light of the moon?

Most often, sacred objects such as these are purchased with good intention and then promptly placed upon an altar or a shelf only to collect dust and the residual energies of the room they live in.

The way in which we employ sacred objects, nurture and care for them does have an impact both on our spiritual practice and our spiritual wellbeing, particularly when those objects are used every so often as a conduit for healing energies, as a portal to life beyond the veil, during meditation or spiritual journeying.

Our sacred objects are in all reality, an extension of us, our integrity and our intention to walk the path of spirit with sincerity.

To metaphysicians, energy healers, shamans, medicine people, mediums, and teachers, I often compare the need to keep our sacred objects cleaned and cared for by asking a simple question:

"If you were going to have surgery on your physical body, would you choose a doctor that keeps their medical instruments meticulously clean and cared for, or one that leaves their dirty scalpels, sponges, scissors, sutures and forceps just sitting on a medical cart for continual use from patient to patient, with no regard to their sanitary condition?"

Without exception, the surgeon who exhibits meticulous care for their instruments is always chosen.

Many, many years ago, after a sacred ceremony, a Lakota holy man shared a long conversation with me about the importance of keeping my sacred objects, such as my prayer pipe, very clean. In doing so, he explained, I am also caring for the *Spirit* of that object.

Keeping *our* body, mind, spirit and emotions cleaned up is an important element to our work with sacred objects, ceremony and healing practices, too. The dirt, grime, dust, emotions and energy that can blanket us, both on our physical body and in our energy body can also collect around and on our special objects.

Incantation to Clear and Recharge Crystals

Holding the crystal(s) in your hands, placing them on a sacred altar or in the energies of direct sun or moonlight is a great way to prepare for reciting this incantation. Placing crystals under gently running water is another option for non-soluble crystals that are safe to place in water.

Incantation to Clear and Recharge Crystals

Father Sun
Mother Moon
Holy Light
please come.

Good and Loving Spirits
of the Crystal, Rock and Mineral Kingdoms,
welcome.

I call upon the brilliant Light of Love
and splendid Healing,
to remove any and all
negative, unhealthy, and unclean,
energies from this crystal.

Thank you for gently placing these energies
deep within the Heart of Creation
to be transformed once again
into luminous, magnificent Light.

Fill this crystal with your love, wisdom, healing and Light.
Make it an instrument of your peace, healing, wisdom, Light and love.
Thank you.
So it is. So be it.

Incantation to Bless a Sacred Object

Holding the sacred object in your hands, placing them on a sacred altar or in the energies of direct sun or moonlight is a great way to prepare for reciting this incantation. Smudging the object with sage/cedar, frankincense/myrrh is also a beautiful companion to this incantation.

Incantation to Bless a Sacred Object

Holy Light,
Loving Light,
Sacred Light of Wisdom,
please come.

Healing Winds of the West,
The North,
The East,
and The South,
please come.

Archangels of Strength,
Boundless Courage,
Abiding Love and Light,
please come.

Bless this sacred object,
and all who employ it,
to do the work of the One Light,
the One Love,
the Source of All Healing,
and Peace,
here on earth.

So it is. So be it.

Incantation to the Faerie Realms

Incantation to the Faerie Realms

Good and Kind Spirits

from the Realms of the Fae,

thank you for your presence in my gardens

and upon the land.

Thank you

for safeguarding the flora and fauna,

and for shielding this space

from all who would

create mischief and imbalance

to the

peacefulness,

joyfulness

wellness

and

love

of

this

place.

So it is.

I am grateful.

Incantation to the Spirit of Love

Incantation to the Spirit of Love

One Love,

Self-Love,

fill me with your peace.

Help me to gently release

all that is unloving from my life.

Eternal Light,

Christed Light,

take from me *all* that is

hateful and harmful to my life.

Beloved Chamuel

Archangel of Love,

thank you for your luminous presence in my life.

Walk with me.

Light of Love,

Spirit of Love,

Sacred Heart and Mind of Love,

please draw near,

and fill me.

Love

now fills me,

walks with me,

and moves through me.

I *am* love and I am *loved.*

So it is.

Incantation to the Ancestors

Incantation to the Ancestors

Ancestors,

I am calling to you.

Old Ones,

I am calling to you.

The named and the nameless,

I am calling to you.

From your home in the stars, the eternal oceans of Life,

speak to me through my bloodline.

Share your stories through my bones.

Visit me in my dreams and visions.

Sing to me, our ancestral songs.

Ancestors,

I thank you for guiding me, loving me, knowing me, and being me.

Old Ones,

I thank you for singing to me, and teaching me with song.

Named Ones and Nameless Ones,

I thank you for holding my Sacred Heart in the eternity of your unending love.

I am grateful.

Entering Your Inner Temple

"Before entering your Inner Temple…

Leave who you *were*

at the door,

and enter with who you *are*."

-Denise Iwaniw-Francisco

Shasta Abbey Buddhist Monastery, Mount Shasta, California USA

Incantation to the Inner Elementals

Incantation to the Inner Elementals

I call to the Healing Spirits of Water,

please, come.

Thank you for cleansing, nourishing and balancing my feelings and emotions.

Help me to walk on calm waters.

I call to the Inspirational Spirits of Air,

please, come.

Thank you for stirring positive, harmonious thoughts within me.

Help me to use right speech.

I call to the Transformational Spirits of Fire,

please, come.

Thank you for lighting my soul's growth with love.

Help me to see the miracles all around and within me.

I call to the Nourishing Spirits of Earth,

please, come.

Thank you for keeping me firmly rooted to my truth.

Help me to stay on my soul's path.

Water, Air, Fire and Earth within me, you are balanced, nourished, inspired and whole.

I am alive!

I am awake!

So it is. So be it.

Incantation to the Four Seasons

Incantation to the Four Seasons

To the Good Spirits of Spring and the East

I bid you welcome.

Eagle, Elk, Ostara, Morning Star Woman and Isis, please come.

Bring your ancient wisdom to this sacred space.

I am Eternal.

To the Good Spirits of Summer and the South

I bid you welcome.

Hawk, Lion, Brigid, Swan Maiden and Cygnus, please come.

Bring your ancient wisdom to this sacred space.

I see with great clarity.

To the Good Spirits of Autumn and the West

I bid you welcome.

Thunderbird, Horse, Evening Star Woman, Cerridwyn and Sirius, please come.

Bring your ancient wisdom to this sacred Space.

I am abundant in all good things.

To the Good Spirits of Winter and the North

I bid you welcome.

Cardinal, Bear, Freya, Ursa Major and Polaris, please come.

Bring your ancient wisdom to this sacred space.

I am divinely guided and protected.

So it is. So be it.

Incantation to the Five Ethers

Incantation to the Five Ethers

I call upon the presence of the Holy Spirit of Water

please come,

and bring your sacred gifts to this space.

I call upon the presence of the Holy Spirit of Air

please come,

and bring your sacred gifts to this space.

I call upon the presence of the Holy Spirit of Fire

please come,

and bring your sacred gifts to this space.

I call upon the presence of the Holy Spirit of Earth

please come,

and bring your sacred gifts to this space.

I call upon the presence of the Holy Spirits

please come,

and bring your sacred gifts to this space.

Holy Spirits of the Water, Air, Fire, Earth and Spirit,

thank you for being present in this sacred space

and for blessing us with your sacred wisdom and healing.

So it is. Blessings be.

The Nine Orders of Angels

Seraphim – These are the closest to the throne of God. They are creatures of pure love and Light.

Cherubim – These are the first angels named in the Hebrew Bible as God stations them at the gates of Eden. The Cherubim are angels of knowledge and glory as well as guardians of the fixed stars. They are also the celestial record keepers.

Angel at Cathedral of the Black Madonna
Rocamadour, France 2014

Thrones – These are the ministering angels of justice. The Thrones are the first group of angels existing closely to the material realm.

Dominions – These angels supervise other angels and oversee the daily happenings of the Universe. Dominions are the guardians of nations.

Virtues – These are the angels of grace and valor. Their primary purpose is to perform miracles on Earth. They intervene and provide courage and strength in humans during moments of great fear and difficulty.

Powers – These are said to be the first angels created by God. They are protectors against evil on Earth and throughout the cosmos.

Principalities – These angels are said to watch over the leaders of nations, helping them to make wise decisions. They are protectors of religion and help humankind maintain their faith.

Archangels – Messengers bearing divine decrees. Michael, Raphael, Gabriel and Uriel.

Angels – These are the angels closest to human beings. They are intermediaries between the heavenly realm and the earthly realm, between the Creator and humans. Angel": From the Greek world "Angelos," a translation of the Hebrew word "Malakh," originally meaning, "Messenger".

Incantation to the Nine Orders of Angels

Incantation to the Nine Orders of Angels

I call to the Blessed Seraphim,

Thank you for bringing the Celestial Fire of Creators cosmic Light to this sacred space.

Divine Cherubim,

Thank you for bringing Divine Knowledge of the galaxies and stars to this sacred space.

Heavenly Thrones,

Thank you for bringing Loving Justice to this sacred space.

Pristine Dominions,

Thank you for bringing Protective Light to this sacred space.

Sacred Virtues,

Thank you for bringing Grace, Valor and Miracles to this sacred space.

Spiritual Powers,

Thank you for protecting this sacred space from all evil.

Virtuous Principalities,

Thank you for bringing balance to this sacred space.

Faithful Archangels,

Thank you for bringing your Legions of Light to this sacred space.

Holy Angels,

Thank you for bringing Universal Grace to this sacred space.

Angels of the Nine Heavenly Realms, thank you for over-lighting this space with your eternal love.

And so it is.

The Four Mighty Archangels

Michael – "Who is like God" or "He who shines like God." He is often referred to as St. Michael, the protector of police officers and soldiers. Michael is the defender of Light and goodness.

Uriel – "Light of God." Uriel brings Divine Light into our lives. Uriel helps us fulfill our dreams and our goals, while helping us to let go and heal the past. Uriel helps to teach us about forgiveness of ourselves and of others.

Gabriel – "Hero of God" or "God is my strength." Gabriel is the angel known for telling the Virgin Mary of her impending birth of Jesus and who later delivered the "Behold, I bring you good tidings of great Joy," news about the newborn Jesus. Gabriel is the messenger who delivered the Koran to Mohammed.

Raphael – "God Heals." Raphael is the angel of all healing. He watches over the healing of the planet earth and those who live upon planet earth. Raphael guides those in the healing arts. Call upon Raphael when you or someone you care for needs healing of the body, mind or spirit. Raphael is also the angel of travelers. As you travel the Mystic Journey, remember to call upon him.

Angels from the Church of the Black Madonna
Rocamadour, France, 2014

Incantation to the Four Mighty Archangels

Incantation to the Four Mighty Archangels
St. Michael, St. Uriel, St. Gabriel, St. Raphael

St. Michael, Archangel of Protection, Defender of Light and Goodness, please come.
Stand at my right-hand side.

St. Uriel, Archangel of Forgiveness, Understanding and Dreams, please come.
Stand before me.

St. Gabriel, Archangel of Aquarius, Fearlessness and Abundant Joy, please come.
Stand at my left-hand side.

St. Raphael, Archangel of Healing, Healers, and Clear Sight, please come.
Stand behind me.

Michael, Uriel, Gabriel, Raphael, thank you for guiding me both day and night.

So it is.

St. Michael's Church, Tintern, Wales, 2016

The Creation of Sacred Waters

The Creation of Sacred Waters

Water is sacred. Water is life. Without it, all things perish. The current of Life that is carried within the intelligence of water is beautifully potent. It is Divine. In sacred ceremonies, water is often employed to ordain, cleanse, baptize, banish, bless and purify.

Many times I have been asked if it is possible for someone other than clergy to create and utilize 'holy water' for ceremonies such as baptism, end of life blessings and the purification of homes and sacred spaces. The answer to that question is, quite simply, "Yes."

Here, I am sharing a very special incantation entitled, "Creating Holy Water." I created this ceremony many years ago and still employ it today.

Remember, you may also place your hands upon yourself to bless the waters within your very own body and psyche.

Creating Holy Water

To create sacred and holy water, place your hands over the vessel of clean water and recite these words:

I call upon the Presence of St. Michael, the Archangel, to bless and infuse this water with your Love and Holy Light.

I call upon the Presence of St. Uriel, the Archangel, to bless and infuse this water with your Love and Holy Light.

I call upon the Presence of St. Gabriel, the Archangel, to bless and infuse this water with your Love and Holy Light.

I call upon the Presence of St. Raphael, the Archangel, to bless and infuse this water with your Love and Holy Light.

I call upon the Presence of Metatron, the Archangel, to bless and infuse this water with your Love and Holy Light.

I call upon the Presence of St. Jophiel, the Archangel, to bless and infuse this water with your Love and Holy Light.

Thank you, Michael, Uriel, Gabriel, Raphael, Metatron and Jophiel for imbuing this water with your Love and Holy Light.

So it is. Amen.

Calling to the Angelics

Calling to the Angelics

The Daily Calling:

I call upon the Archangel St. Michael,

I call upon the Archangel St. Uriel,

I call upon the Archangel St. Raphael,

I call upon the Archangel St. Gabriel,

I call upon the Archangel Metatron,

I call upon the Archangel Raziel,

Angels of Light, thank you for protecting, guiding and Lighting my way,

Each moment of my life.

The Daily Clearing:

St. Michael, Archangel of the 7th Heavenly Realm

and the Legions of Light,

Thank you for clearing *any* and *all* negativity from every nook and cranny

of this building (or home, etc.)

Thank you for ushering all dark forces back to the Light,

and for filling this building (or home, etc.)

with the loving Light of God.

Care of the Soul

"When we take the time to *care* for our soul, we are, in effect, *nurturing* our *entire* world. We must *choose* to love ourselves!

When we take the time to *hear* the voice of our soul, we are, in fact, *listening* to the voice of Spirit, that dances deep *within* and all *around us. Choose* to dance along!

When we take the time to *express* the wondrously unique *gifts* of our soul, we are in essence, shining our *Light* on earth.

Choose to shine!"

-Denise Iwaniw-Francisco

Egyptian children waving as we make our way to Abydos Temple in Egypt, 2009

Chakras

Chakras

Aligning your spiritual and physical bodies is about equalizing the energy in and around your body. This energy is known as the "chakra" system and the "aura". Chakra is a Sanskrit word meaning "wheels of energy". These wheels of energy are located along your spine, your forehead and the top of your head. Your aura field is the field of energy, which surrounds or encases your entire body.

The most common teachings regarding chakras center on the philosophy of seven chakra centers located along your body's energy meridians. They are from bottom to top:

1st Chakra – Color: Red Located at the base of the spine. This energy center represents your seat of security and survival. It connects you to Mother Earth and is home to Kundalini energy. Burning some cedar or clove essential oil will enhance and balance this chakra.

2nd Chakra – Color: Orange Located just below the navel. This energy center represents creativity – procreation, sexuality, and is the center through which 'clear feeling' or clairsentience enters our consciousness. Burning some ylang-ylang or sandalwood will help enhance and balance this chakra.

3rd Chakra – Color: Yellow Located just above the navel. This energy center represents our will, autonomy and self-esteem. Burning some lavender, rosemary and bergamot essential oils will help enhance and balance this chakra.

4th Chakra – Color: Green Located in the heart center. This energy center represents the energy of love. The love that we have for ourselves and the love that we have for others. This is the chakra of compassion. Burning some Rose essential oil will help enhance and balance this chakra.

5th Chakra – Color: Sky blue Located at the base of the throat. This energy center is about 'speaking our truth'. It is also the center through which 'clear hearing' or clairaudience enters our consciousness. Burning some sage or eucalyptus essential oils will help enhance and balance this chakra.

6th Chakra – Color: Indigo Located in the center of the forehead. This energy center is about 'seeing things clearly'. It is the center through which 'clear seeing' or clairvoyance enters our consciousness. Burning some mint or jasmine essential oils will help enhance and balance this chakra.

7th Chakra – Color: Purple, Silver, and Gold Located at the crown of the head. This energy center is the gateway and our connection to the Divine. Seen as a golden halo or aura in many forms of sacred art, this seventh chakra is our connection to our Divine Home. Burning olibanum or lotus essential oils will help enhance and balance this chakra.

By visualizing each of your chakras, beginning at the base of your spine and moving gently upward, vibrantly spinning in perfect balance, you help to keep your wheels of energy in perfect alignment. Being in balance helps you receive, understand and then act upon psychic guidance. You can also maintain balance by drinking a lot of water, eating healthy food and getting plenty of rest. All of these things help keep your psychic 'antenna' clean and in perfect operating condition.

Protecting Your Energy Body

Because our aura can become cluttered with the emotions, problems and outside psychic influences (psychic attack) of others throughout our day, an easy way to keep your aura clean is to take a bath in Epsom salts before bed. Be sure to get your head wet too. This way, negative energy doesn't simply move upward, causing a nasty headache! By adding a little lavender to your bath, not only is your aura cleaned, but it is also relaxed.

Envisioning your body and aura completely surrounded by crystal white light during the day is an excellent way to protect yourself from low vibrations as well. Keeping a piece of black obsidian nearby will also help to absorb negativity. Just as you can smudge a room to clear negativity, you can also smudge your body and your aura. After lighting a high vibration incense or sage/sweet grass in a fire safe burner, allow the smoke to begin to billow out of the burner. As it does, fan the billowing smoke with a feather so that you in effect, bathe yourself in the essence of the incense.

Ultimately, always remember that 'like attracts like'. If you indulge in high vibration activities such as positive speech, meditation, prayer, volunteer work, and group activities involving people of integrity, you will continue to attract high vibration experiences in your life. The positive energy that you exude in your thoughts or daily activities will come back to you as positive energy in the form of positive experiences, people and abundance. Likewise, when we spend our time in the company of people of less integrity who spend much of their time gossiping, living in a constant state of fear, greed, complaining, using illegal substances and hanging out in low vibration places, we will continue to attract those experiences in our lives. When we put forth negative energy, we shall attract negativity in return. Distancing ourselves from these people and activities will increase our vibration and heighten our ability to ward off psychic attack and negativity in our lives.

Incantation to the Seven Chakras

Incantation to the Seven Chakras

Bring your attention to each of your seven chakra centers as you recite this incantation and remember to breathe deeply and exhale between each chakra invocation.

I call to the Infinite Light of the Rainbow Galaxies that exist within the vast expanse of the Cosmos, and live deep inside of me, to balance, heal, nurture and strengthen my energy bodies:

Holy Intelligence of my Base Chakra

you are now balanced, centered and whole. I AM secure.

Creative Intelligence of my Second Chakra

you are now balanced, centered and whole. I AM creative.

Solar Intelligence of my Third Chakra

you are now balanced, centered and whole. I AM intuitive.

Loving Intelligence of my Fourth Chakra

you are now balanced, centered and whole. I AM loved.

Sacred Intelligence of my Fifth Chakra

you are now balanced, centered and whole. I have ears to hear.

Divine Intelligence of my Sixth Chakra

you are now balanced, centered and whole. I have eyes to see.

Heavenly Intelligence of my Seventh Chakra

you are now balanced, centered and whole. Creator and I are one.

Six pointed star of the White Eagle Lodge, London, England 2012

Incantation to the Divine Intelligence Within My Body

Incantation to the Divine Intelligence Within My Body

(As you recite each stanza, visualize the body part(s)
that you are calling to, seeing them in perfect health).

I call to the Divine Intelligence within all of my organs.
You are nourished, healthy, balanced and whole.

I call to the Divine Intelligence within my bones.
You are strong, healthy, balanced and whole.

I call to the Divine Intelligence within my flesh.
You are healthy, nourished, balanced and whole.

I call to the Divine Intelligence within my muscles.
You are healthy, nourished, balanced and whole.

I call to the Divine Intelligence within my blood.
You are healthy, nourished, balanced and whole.

I call to the Divine Intelligence within my eyes.
You are healthy, nourished, balanced and whole.

I call to the Divine Intelligence within my brain.
You are healthy, nourished, balanced and whole.

I call to the Divine Intelligence within my _____(fill in with your own intention).
You are healthy, nourished, balanced and whole.

My body is healthy, nourished, balanced and whole.

I AM healthy, nourished, balanced, joyful, grateful and whole.

So it is! Blessings be!

Incantation to My Higher Self and Soul

Incantation to My Higher Self and Soul

Soul body, I call to you.

Please come.

Higher Self, I call to you.

Please come.

Adorn me in your forever and ancient wisdom.

Wrap me in the gossamer of your Divine Love.

Infuse my body, mind, emotions and Spirit with your pristine Nature;

the Heart and Mind of God and Goddess.

Let us walk this Earth Journey as One.

Inseparable.

Eternally awake and aware,

that You are me

and I am You;

as it was in Our beginning and forever shall be.

So it is.

So be it.

A feathered sentry at Stonehenge, England 2016

Don't Look Back

"Rather than look *back,*

look at just how far you've come!

Celebrate the lessons

that Life has taught you

along the Way!

Each of them

has served to make you

the beautiful *Light*

that you have become."

-Denise Iwaniw-Francisco

The inlet waters at Merlin's Cave, Tintagel, England, 2016

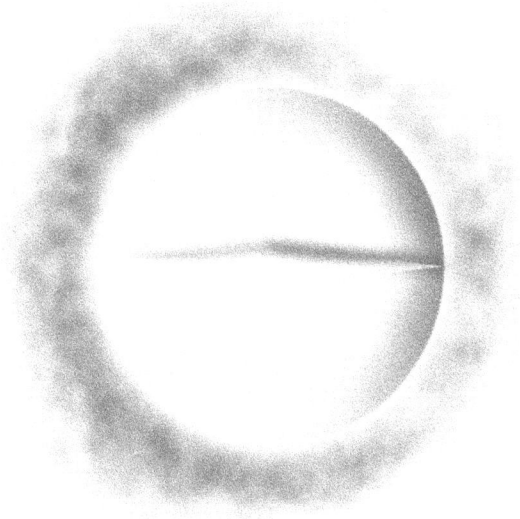

Prayers and Ceremonies for Rites of Passage

Forest Stairway to the Cave Church of St. Mary Magdalene, Saint Baume, France, 2014

Prayer for a Baptismal Rite

Prayer for a Baptismal Rite

Words to the baptized:

"You are a splendid Child of Light, a living expression of God.

May your life be blessed by the love of the Holy Mother, and the Divine Father, and your journey be guided by the unending love of Creation, overseen by the myriad realms of the Angels of Light and filled with abundant joys and deep, abiding peace."

Holy Mother,

Divine Father,

Holy Spirit,

we are here before you this day, acknowledging our many blessings,

and your heavenly presence in the life of this child,

brought before you

to be baptized in the Light and Wisdom

of your eternal Love.

May each of our lives, as that of this child,

be touched by your grace,

nurtured by your tenderness,

and filled with the harmony and joy of the Holy Spirit.

So it is.

Amen.

Prayer for Welcoming a Child to Their Earthly Journey

Prayer for Welcoming a Child to Their Earthly Journey

(Name of Child) welcome to Grandmother Earth,

and to the holy human journey of your magnificent Soul.

You came here to shine as only *you* can shine.

Let your radiant Light shine!

Beautiful, living expression of the Creator,

imbued with exquisite gifts and talents,

we welcome you.

Your life,

and every ounce of your being,

is celebrated.

Sing your songs. Dance your dances. Brings your Souls' Dream to life.

Remember beloved, that you are wise.

You are ancient.

You are holy.

You are eternal.

You are safe.

You are love.

And, you are loved.

Welcome.

Blessings be.

Prayer to Bless a Child

To Bless a Child

I call upon the Presence of Archangel St. Michael,

Angel of Courage and Defender of the Light.

I call upon the Presence of Archangel St. Uriel,

Angel of Guidance and Perpetual Light.

I call upon the Presence of Archangel St. Raphael,

Angel of Healing and Balance.

I call upon the Presence of Archangel St. Gabriel.

Angel of Strength and Fortitude.

Thank you, Archangels of Light, for over-lighting the life of (Insert name of Child).

Thank you for guiding her/his steps and for protecting her/him from all harm.

Creator of all things, thank you for the gift of this child,

and the opportunity to love, care for and to nurture them here on earth.

Amen.

Sacred Water from the Lion's Head Fountain at the Chalice Well, Glastonbury, England, 2016

Naming Ceremony

Naming Ceremony

(A ceremony for newborns, adopted children and adults)

Beloved, beautiful child,

always remember that you

are a divine reflection and expression

of the love and Light of God.

In the presence of your Guardian Angels, your ancestors, family and friends,

we have gathered to present you with your sacred shield, your name.

From this moment forward, you will be known as _____.

(Sharing the meaning of someone's name is a powerful addition to this ceremony. If being named after

someone you may wish to take a moment to share this. If the name is chosen for

another special reason, please take a moment to share this as well.)

Together, we celebrate your loving presence in our lives.

We celebrate the beauty of your hopes and the brilliance of your dreams.

We honor your unique gifts and talents,

and we support you in their expression upon the Earth plane.

Let us all welcome <u>(insert name)</u>.

Blessings be.

A Fairy Tree in Glendolough, Ireland, 2016

End of Life and Funeral Rites

Our Lady of Provence, France 2014

Celebration of Life Ceremony

Celebration of Life

Welcome:

Blessings to all who have gathered in the beautiful, sacred space.

We welcome the presence of the Archangel St. Michael,

the Archangel St. Uriel,

the Archangel St. Gabriel,

and the Archangel St. Raphael,

to over-light and imbue this gathering

with the Light and the Love of the Creator.

The origin of our soul is holy. It is sacred. From our Home in spirit, our holy and sacred soul *chooses* to incarnate within the confines of flesh and bones. Each of us desires to experience humanness while expressing the Light of our sacred Source right here on Grandmother Earth. We are *holy* beings, called to *shine* and experience being wholly human.

Today, we come together to celebrate the Light and the life of

_____.

Born on (Birthdate), (Name of deceased), lived a life dedicated to:
(Insert a list of family, friends, the, passions, hobbies, etc. of the deceased).

On (Insert date of death), Creator tenderly welcomed (Name of deceased) back Home; a place of unending love where ancestors and angels gathered to celebrate their return.

Eulogies:

Let's take a moment to share fond memories of our time together with (Name of the deceased) here on Earth: (Welcome those present to step forward and share a beautiful memory). Sharing poems, songs or thoughts that have been written about the loved one is also a beautiful way to pay tribute to a life well lived.

Conclusion:

Heavenly Father, Divine Mother, thank you for the gift of life, for the gift of one another and for the gift of your eternal and unconditional love.

Together, we thank you for the life of (Name of deceased) and for welcoming (her/him) Home to the heavens, where we will one day see and embrace one another again. We thank the Angels of Light for accompanying (Name of deceased) on this journey, and for comforting friends and family who are left to celebrate (her/his) life and to mourn (her/his) passing.

May peaceful blessings be upon and within each and every one of us, as we leave this sacred space. Let us carry the love of the Creator and the love of (Name of deceased) forever in our hearts and shine it outward into the world.

Eagle head cloud over Porcupine, South Dakota, 2010

"Your loved ones want you to be happy. They want you to go on. Life without them will be a different life, but you must go back to your life and not hold them to earth with your tears."

-Chris Eagle Hawk, Lakota Elder

at Wiping of the Tears Ceremony, Oglala, South Dakota

Dullknife Family Pow Wow and Gathering 2017

Prayer for the Journey Home

The Journey Home

I call upon the Archangel St. Michael,

I call upon the Archangel St. Uriel,

I call upon the Archangel St. Raphael,

I call upon the Archangel St. Gabriel.

Archangels of Light, thank you for accompanying the Spirit of our loved one Home.

Thank you for guiding their transition from the physical realm on earth

back to the realms of Light and Love,

where the Creator dwells.

Thank you for helping them to celebrate the beautiful friendships

and family ties that they helped to create.

Thank you for helping them to know that their life on earth was a gift to many.

Amen.

Kaduval Temple Gardens, Kauai 2017

Prayer for Homecoming

Homecoming

Holy Mother, Divine Father,

Creator of *all* that is,

all that has ever been,

and *all* that shall ever be,

thank you for the gift of this precious life.

In the beginning, we became.

With a love unlike any other, You joyfully breathed our Soul into existence;

each of us a holy and sacred reflection of You.

During the course of a human lifetime,

we don the apparel of flesh and bones

and are called to love one another,

as You love us;

bringing heaven to earth.

In physical death, we shed the cloak of our humanity

and our eternal Spirit returns to the Love of You.

Forever living,

Perpetually expressing,

infinitely loving,

always experiencing,

and brightly shining

from Home;

which is You.

So it is.

Amen.

Upon the Four Winds I Commend Your Spirit

Upon the Four Winds I Commend Your Spirit

I call to the Winds of the West;

home of the Ancestors.

Ancestors, please come.

I call to the Winds of the North:

home of the Ancestral Songs.

Sing this beloved Spirit Home.

I call to the Winds of the East;

home of the Eagle.

Eagle Nation, help this mighty Spirit to soar.

I call to the Winds of the South;

home of Infinite Light.

Welcome back to the Light, this eternal Soul.

Into your care,

I place this loved one.

Tenderly return them

to the unending Light of all Creation.

Safely guard,

guide,

and deliver

this beautiful one

Home.

Amen.

Prayer for the Passing of a Beloved Pet

Prayer for the Passing of a Beloved Pet

Archangels of Light

Good and loving Spirits of Nature,

thank you for accompanying the Spirit of our loved one Home.

Thank you for guiding their transition from the physical realm on earth

back to the realms of Light and Love,

where the Creator dwells.

Creator of All Things

good, loving and kind.

The two-legged, four-legged,

the winged ones,

the swimmers,

and the creepy crawlers,

thank you for the precious gift of this relative.

I am grateful for the life, love and friendship

of this beautiful being,

and joyful in the knowledge that one day

we shall be together again,

within the Heart and Love of You.

Amen.

Life

In the Beginning

Bright Star Blessings to all who read these words and to those with whom these words are shared...

In the beginning, *all* things emanated Angelic Light

In the beginning, were you.

In the end, all things Angelic return to the One Home.

In the end, The One Home is where you shall return.

Between the beginning and the end, you are asked to play … to dance … to sing … to make a joyful noise.

Between the beginning and the end, you are asked to share your unique Light emanation with the world.

The stars above, reflect your radiant starlight within. Shine, like the vast expanse of the

cosmos!

The sun above, shines warmly and brightly in you. Radiate the warmth of the Creator like never before!

The moon above, glows like the ancient wisdom you contain. Share your knowledge with the world!

In the beginning...emanated all things Angelic, who came to earth to play, to sing, to dance and to make a joyful noise. They came to share their unique Light with all of creation, shining like the Sun, reflecting like Stars and glowing like the Moon...before returning to the One Home, where joyful homecoming celebrations are had and golden badges of courage are bestowed, by those Angelic emanations who have gone before and those who hope for the privilege to one day go.

In the beginning, in between, and in the end...are you.

-St. Israfel Archangel of the Hero's Journey

A Love Letter from the Archangel St. Israfel, "A Year of Mystic Angels" by Denise Iwaniw

Searching for Home

"From the moment that we are born,

we begin the process of dying,

and our return to Home,

which is Love.

That pure, unconditional Love,

that we sometimes call the *Light*.

As with all things that are finding their way *Home*,

each of us looks for signs along the way

that tell us Home is somewhere near.

So it is,

that the moment we take our first breath in human form,

our search for *Love,*

which is Home,

begins."

-Denise Iwaniw-Francisco

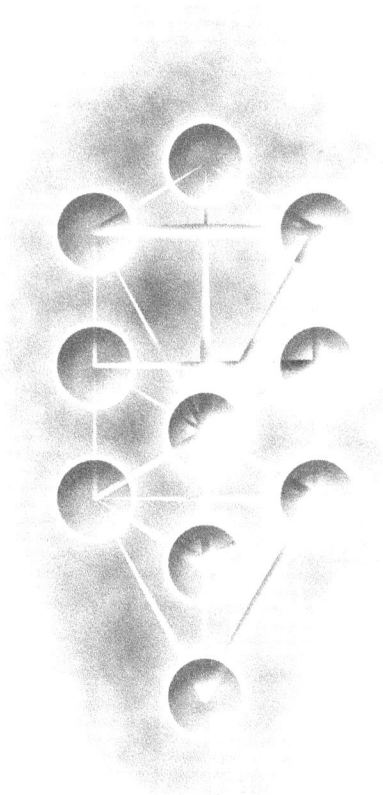

Weddings and Partnership Rites

Ancient Cairn at Newgrange, Ireland, 2016

Ceremony of Sacred Union

Sacred Union

Officiant:

Welcome family and friends to the union of (Insert names of those being wed).

Together, let us create a sacred and loving space for this ceremony:

I call upon the Archangel St. Michael,

I call upon the Archangel St. Uriel,

I call upon the Archangel St. Raphael,

I call upon the Archangel St. Gabriel,

Thank you, Archangels of Light, for over-lighting this ceremony of sacred union between

(Insert names of those being united).

Thank you for your joyful presence here and for shining your Light upon all who have

gathered.

Officiant says to those gathered: "Let us surround (insert names of the couple) with our love, as they take the vows of sacred union."

"(Insert names of the couple), look at each other and remember always this moment in time. Now you will share words that will take you across a new threshold in life and things will never be quite the same between the two of you. After these words are spoken you shall forever say to the world, this is my beloved."

Reading of the vows: (Officiant invites the couple to face one another and to recite their

individual vows to the other).

Sealing of the vows by officiant: "I will ask you now to seal these vows you have just made by the giving and receiving of the wedding rings."

Officiant: "May I have the rings please?"

Blessing and exchange of the rings by officiant:

"The wedding ring has been a traditional symbol of commitment and enduring love that, like a circle, has no end. These rings are your gift to each other; they are the outward and visible signs of an inward and spiritual bond that unites your two hearts in love that has no end."

Officiant (addressing the groom):

"Please repeat after me while placing this ring on (insert name of bride) finger:"

"(Insert name of bride) this ring is an outward symbol of my love for you. It represents the sacred union of my soul to yours.

Officiant (addressing the bride):

"Please repeat after me while placing this ring on (insert name of groom) finger:"

"(Insert name of groom), this ring is an outward of my love for you. It represents the sacred union of my soul to yours."

Officiant closes the ceremony with:

Creator of *all* things, thank you for the gift of this couple and the opportunity to witness their love here on earth.

Lead them down abundant pathways, and joyful trails.

Help them to celebrate the uniqueness of each other and the blessing of their relationship.

Thank you for helping them to grow alongside one another and together as a team.

Bless their home, their lives and their love with your love. Amen.

Officiant addressing the couple:

"You have openly declared your wishes to be united as one and in the presence of family and friends, have pledged your love to one another."

"Family and friends, it is my pleasure to present to you, (insert the names of the couple), now joined in sacred union."

Wedding Ceremony

A Wedding

Welcome by the officiant:

Let us begin by welcoming the presence of Creator within each of us.

Let us surround (Insert names of the couple) with our love, our prayers and our best wishes for them on this, their wedding day, and throughout their journey together as husband and wife.

We welcome the presence of the Four Winds and the Mighty Archangels:

St. Michael, Archangel

St. Uriel, Archangel

St. Raphael, Archangel

St. Gabriel, Archangel

(Insert names of the couple), look at each other and remember always this moment in time. Now you will share words that will take you across a new threshold in life and things will never be quite the same between the two of you. After these words are spoken you shall forever say to the world, this is my husband and this is my wife.

Reading of the Vows: (Officiant invites the couple to recite their individual vows to one another).

Sealing of the vows by officiant: "I will ask you now to seal these vows you have just made by the giving and receiving of the wedding rings."

Officiant: "May I have the rings please?"

Blessing and Exchange of the rings by officiant:

"The wedding ring has been a traditional symbol of commitment and enduring love that, like a circle, has no end. These rings are your gift to each other; they are the outward and visible signs of an inward and spiritual bond that unites your two hearts in love that has no end."

Officiant (addressing the groom):

"Please repeat after me while placing this ring on (insert name of bride) finger:"

"(Insert name of bride) this ring is a token of my love. I marry you with this ring, with all that I have and all that I am."

Officiant (addressing the bride):

"Please repeat after me while placing this ring on (insert name of groom) finger:"

"(Insert name of groom), this ring is a token of my love. I marry you with this ring, with all that I have and all that I Am."

Officiant addressing the couple:

"You have openly declared your wishes to be united in marriage, and in the presence of family and friends, have pledged your love to one another. By the power of your love and commitment and by the power vested in me by the State of _____, I now pronounce you husband and wife."

"Groom … you may kiss your wife!"

"Bride … you may kiss your husband!"

"Family and friends, it is my pleasure to present to you, (insert the names of the couple), now joined as husband and wife!"

Invitation to the Angels of Love

Invitation to the Angels of Love

Welcome to this sacred space,

and sacred union,

the Angels of Light and Love.

Archangel St. Michael,

Angel of Courage and Strength.

Archangel St. Uriel,

Angel of Perpetual Light.

Archangel St. Gabriel,

Angel of Gentleness and Knowing.

Archangel St. Raphael,

Angel of Healing and Health.

Archangel Metatron,

Angel of Ancient Wisdom.

Archangel Jophiel,

Angel of Ecstatic Union.

Archangel Chamuel,

Angel of Eternal Love.

Welcome.

Thank you for over-lighting this sacred union of souls

and this ceremony of love.

Amen.

Calling to the Winds of Union

Calling to the Winds of Union

I call to the Winds of the East,

the winds of new beginnings.

Bless this couple with the knowledge

that each new day is an opportunity to expand their love.

I call to the Winds of the South,

the winds of vitality and joy.

Bless this couple with the wisdom to know

that laughter is good medicine and keeps a loving relationship healthy and strong.

I call to the Winds of the West,

the winds of the ancestors and ancestral songs.

Bless this couple with the knowledge that those who have gone before them

stand with them and love them from beyond.

I call to the Winds of the North,

the winds of strength and endurance.

Bless this couple with the wisdom to know

that the greatest trials are often the catalyst to the greatest love.

I call to the Winds of the Star Nations,

the winds of cosmic eternity.

Bless this couple with the understanding that they are eternal

and that this human life is but a blink of an eye, in whole of Creation.

I call to the winds of the Holy Spirits,

the winds of Spiritual Wisdom.

Bless this couple with the awareness

that their Souls have chosen this sacred and holy union. Love one another. Amen.

Epilogue

Della Badwound, Lakota Elder, editing this manuscript, August, 2017

It is here that I would like to thank my dear friends and editors, Lillian Cosme, Dinah Gerard, Sharon Rosenblum and my husband Todd Francisco for gifting my work with their expertise as wordsmiths and literary mechanics. I feel your exquisite presence within each of the pages of this book and I am so grateful. Thank you for journeying with me in this precious lifetime. Thank you for being part of my journey.

My 'čhuwéku', elder sister, Della Badwound is pictured here, editing the Lakota Sioux language within the manuscript. 'Philámayaye' I thank you, sister for helping to make sure that my use of the language is correct.

In order to take the magnificent photos of us that are contained within the pages and upon the cover of this book, photographer Nicole Werner spent many hours in the Michigan winter cold to photograph me, my horses and my daughter, Elyse. Thank you, Nicole, for sharing your extraordinary gifts as a make-up artist and photographer. Your ability to capture the magic, passion and love of life on film is simply breathtaking. Thank you for being part of my life.

Artist David Fix not only designed this incredibly beautiful book cover and perfected the layout of its interior, he also graced the entirety of this work with his vision and deep connection to the Divine. He 'sees' my work and is inspired to create from what his soul perceives. Thank you for sharing your gifts with me, David. Thank you for being part of my soul's path.

My beautiful friends, Esoteric Egyptologist and Coptic Minister, Ortrun Franklin, and Mervyn Kelly from the Order of Bards, Ovates and Druids, in the United Kingdom, took the time to read this manuscript in its raw form and then share their honest thoughts, perceptions and feelings about it from their knowledgeable perspectives. Thank you Ortrun and Mervyn for sharing the gift of your ancient wisdom with me. Thank you for being part of my soul's evolution.

To my countless readers, students and clients who continue to shine their magnificent Light, and share their astonishing gifts around Grandmother Earth … please know that *each* of you are precious to me and to my soul's incredible journey. This experience of being human is more beautiful because of you. Thank you for walking alongside me on this great adventure called life.

The human journey, to me, is a grand experience that our soul has chosen to undertake. It is an epic adventure that is blessed with moments of love, passion, joy, pain, trials, and triumphs, and in the end, a celebratory return to our one *true* Home. Simultaneously, it is in the process of experiencing what it is to be a human being that we can find ourselves in a state of forgetfulness, forever reaching toward wholeness, and sometimes quenching our thirst for divine love in all the wrong places.

Our infinite soul knows fully that during our earthly adventure, we are able to catch only glimpses of the vastness and indescribable beauty from which we came. When we take the time to quiet ourselves, to listen to the voice of our soul, and follow its divine guidance, we are able to tap into, and *rejoin* those glorious places that reside in the heavenly realms outside and within us.

The human body that we inhabit is truly a gift, a sacred temple and a vehicle through which our soul is able to shine our own *unique* Light here on earth. Love yourself as you love others. Be good to yourself as you are good to others. If you are struggling, be gentle with yourself just as you are gentle with others who struggle. Encourage yourself to shine your gifts and talents upon the earth, as you encourage others to do the same. Shine your brilliant Light in the darkened places, the hungry places, the ignorant places, the sorrowful places, the fearful places, the hateful places. Shine your Light in *all* places.

You are, after all, a precious being of Love and Light who has embarked upon a heroic journey to share that very same Love and Light upon this cosmic outpost known as Grandmother Earth.

In great joy,

Dana

Denise Iwaniw-Francisco is an accomplished author, spiritual teacher and owner of The Temple Within LLC and The Temple Within School of Sacred Studies. She lectures and teaches in the U.S. and abroad in a variety of areas, encompassing the practices of spiritual development and balanced living. A sought after guest lecturer at colleges and universities, Denise shares her wisdom regarding spiritual pathways and the life journey with an open heart and gentle humor. Denise has written several highly successful books and produced many guided visualization audios.

Todd and Me in Tintagel, England 2016

A native of Georgia, Denise now resides in Michigan, along with her husband Todd and their adult children. Together with their dogs, paint horses and the various woodland animals that live with them at their home in the forest, they have affectionately named their many acres, The Enchanted Forest.

Co-owner of The Mystic's Heart, Denise has released the highly popular Empowerment Deck oracle card series with artist, David Fix. The Mystic Angels, Mysteries of Ancient Egypt, Animal Spirit Totems and the Spirit of Mythology Empowerment Decks are now enjoyed in over 60 countries worldwide. In 2017, Denise and David began to create and release their much anticipated series of spiritual books for children.

Dedicated to the preservation of Native American culture, languages and spirituality, Denise is the founder and president of Gathering Thunder Foundation.

To learn more about Denise and to order her books, CDs, audio courses and oracle decks, please visit her at her DeniseIwaniw.com

Notes

Notes

Notes

Notes